BEING a GIRL

HAYLEY LONG

ILLUSTRATED by GEMMA CORRELL

Andrews McMeel
Publishing®

a division of Andrews McMeel Universal

CONTENTS

This book is for you.
That's right, YOU.

Chapter 1
BEING A GIRL

Being a girl is awesome.

And being a teenage girl is especially awesome.

For one thing, you're not yet a full-fledged adult, and this is **good**. It means that no one can reasonably expect you to behave like Ms. Matilda Mature for hours and hours on end. But at the same time, you're not a little kid any more either. And this is **good** too. Because no one can reasonably expect you to wear that daisy cardigan that was lovingly hand-knitted for you by your grandma.

And when you're a teenage girl, you have plenty of time to do the things that you really **want** to be doing. Like sleeping and chatting and listening to loud music and sleeping and shopping and wearing cool clothes and sleeping and chatting and laughing so hard that it makes you cry and sleeping and dreaming and being a bit random.

And when you're a teenage girl, you don't have to worry about the boring stuff. Like having a full-time job and paying bills.

All in all, it's a unique and special situation that you're in.

Happy days!

So why waste your precious teenage time reading this book?

Shouldn't you just be living the teenage dream?

The answer is yes and no. Live the dream, definitely. But spare a couple of hours to read this book too. There's a good chance you might get something useful out of it. Because even though **your age alone** makes you one of planet Earth's **bright young things**, being a teenage girl *isn't* a nonstop bundle of LOLs.

Sometimes it's actually quite strange and baffling and **seriously weird**.

And every once in a while, it's just a total headache. Which you probably already know.

On those headache days, you might catch yourself wishing you'd been born a boy. But if you think that boys have it easy, just take a moment to consider these two things:

1. **The smell of your bedroom**. I bet it smells nice. Am I right? Now think of your brother's bedroom.* Enough said.

2. **Male bodies are weird**. I'm not being rude. I'm being factual. There's no point denying it—the penis is a pretty peculiar apparatus. It has its uses, of course. In fact, it can do some marvelous things. But, be honest, would you **really** want a penis of your own?

Nope. Me neither.

---

* No brother? No problem. Just find a spare room in your house and throw in some wet grass, a couple of hamsters, several scoops of mashed potatoes, and a pair of sweaty soccer cleats. Then take a long hard sniff. If you did have a brother, there's a good chance that this is what his room would smell like—more or less.

Still wish you were a boy?

If the answer is yes, **please don't panic**—you're not the first and you certainly won't be the last. These things happen. It's because **gender** is something that is thrust upon us whether we like it or not. A bit like a weird birthday present. Or that hand-knitted daisy cardigan. I'll talk more about gender a little later on.

If the answer is **not** yes but

NO WAY

. . . then **welcome back to the sisterhood**, my friend. Being a girl is something worth celebrating. It means you're

young

and

EXCITING

and

packed with possibilities.

And, OK, there are those awkward moments. And other sorts of weirdness too—but here's the thing:

You don't need to go through any of the bad parts on your own.

Because if there's **one thing** that all of us girls tend to be pretty good at, **it's talking about how we feel**. And that's really handy. Because it means that some girl somewhere—whether it's your best friend or your sympathetic sister or your trustworthy aunt or just some random woman who's written a letter to a magazine—will know **exactly** how you feel and be happy to share the experience with you. This will make that awkward moment seem less bad and more normal. But just in case you still think that **NOBODY** understands and you're in this totally on your own—you're not! You've got **me** and I'm talking to you via this book!

But who the heck am I?

I write stuff for teenagers, and my mission here is to steer you through all of life's harsher moments and tell you **everything I know** about being a girl. And I know a thing or two because:

1. I've been one.

2. I'm currently a woman.* Which is the same as being a girl, really— just older.

3. In addition to being a writer, I was an English teacher for years—and this means I've chatted with teenage girls about every subject under the sun. That's the beauty of books for you! They're full of all sorts of delicious details that lead to all sorts of fascinating discussions. Shakespeare's plays are the best. Because his favorite topics are pretty much these:

SEX, DEATH
&
BETRAYAL

* I'm not expecting this situation to change.

By the way, do you know how old Juliet was when she snuck off in secret to marry her Romeo? Thirteen.

Thirteen!

So if you ever hear anyone ranting about how the young people of today are getting worse, quietly ignore them. They are wrong. Please feel free to use Romeo and Juliet as evidence.

4. I've talked to a bunch of boys as well. This means I have **inside information**. I can tell you a bit about **what boys think**.

Also, I promise not to talk to you as if you're a toddler with a mouthful of Goldfish crackers—I'll tell it to you straight.

But before we go any further, I'm going to let you in on a personal secret. I was terrible at being a teenage girl.

TERRIBLE.

Or I thought I was. And if I could travel back in time and tell the thirteen-year-old me that one day I'd be trusted with the important task of writing this book, I'd laugh really hard in my own middle-aged face and say:

No one will ever let me write a book like that. I don't even wear a bra yet!

And this sad fact was perfectly true. Which is why I thought I was terrible at being a teenage girl.

Terrible *smerrible.*

The truth

What you are about to read next is probably the most important sentence I have ever written.

There is no right way to be a girl or wrong way to be a girl.

Just make sure you're being a fairly decent human being and you'll be just fine.

OK, let's get going.

So it's easy, then? There's no possible way to get this **girl** thing wrong?

Hmm. Not exactly.

When you reach a certain age, being a girl is actually really **complicated**. You've probably already discovered this for yourself.

It starts getting complicated the second that we're plopped out into the world. Maybe even before that. Maybe it actually begins the moment the doctor or nurse or midwife points at a fuzzy blob on a computer screen—the blob is **you**, by the way—and says, "Oooh, it's going to be a girl."*

Because that's when **The Pressure** starts.

I need to pause here to introduce my **Student Focus Group**. This is a group of roughly sixty high school juniors and seniors—boys and girls—who helpfully chatted with me about their experiences growing up. The girls also wrote down answers to the following three questions:

1. **What are the three best things about being a girl?**

2. **What are the three worst things about being a girl?**

3. **What advice would you give to your thirteen-year-old self?**

Here are some of the responses to question 2.

- pressure to look good

Pressure to look good is overwhelming

PRESSURE TO BE
ANYONE EXCEPT YOURSELF

Pressure to be 'girly' + pretty

• Pressure to have a 'boyfriend'

---

* If you're reading this and you happen to be a boy or a man, it's unlikely that anyone ever said this. But let me take this opportunity to CONGRATULATE YOU right now on being cool enough and curious enough to read a book called Being a Girl. Thank you, sir. I salute you.

Notice a pattern? Yep, it's the P-word.* It cropped up again and again and again.

So where the heck is all this **pressure** coming from?

Well, this is where we come to something really important . . .

Gender and identity

People belong to lots of groups. They sometimes join little ones like an art club or a sports team or the Girl Scouts. And other groups just claim them as members anyway. These are the big ones. Like working class or middle class. And being American or Mexican or Korean. And being Black or Asian or Jewish or Muslim as well. All these groups can be called communities or societies. And the biggest one encompasses all of these and doesn't need any extra labeling or explanation. It just gets called society.

Society has a view on **everything**. It certainly has a view on what a girl is. So the moment our sex is discovered, society starts bombarding us with messages about how we should look and behave. These messages are sent to us through television, magazines, books, films, and also by our family and friends. The reason **why** we get these messages is very complicated—but it's mostly a souvenir from the olden days when boys needed to fight woolly mammoths and wildebeests, and girls needed to stay in the cave and look after babies.

In very basic terms, it works something like this:

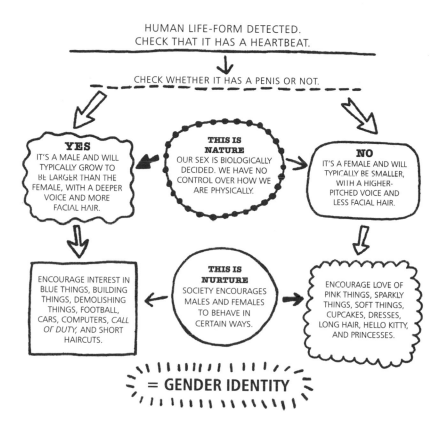

This system of **nature + nurture = gender identity** works as comfortably as clockwork for some people but it also creates a lot of pressure for others. In fact, most of us will feel like we're under some sort of pressure at some stage in our lives—because **we aren't always that interested in** the things we're told we **should** like. And maybe we don't **look** how we think we should, either. This experience of feeling a bit stressed and a bit different is very common. So if pink, sparkly things aren't your bag, don't sweat it. Cheerfully pull on your camouflage cargo pants instead. You aren't alone.

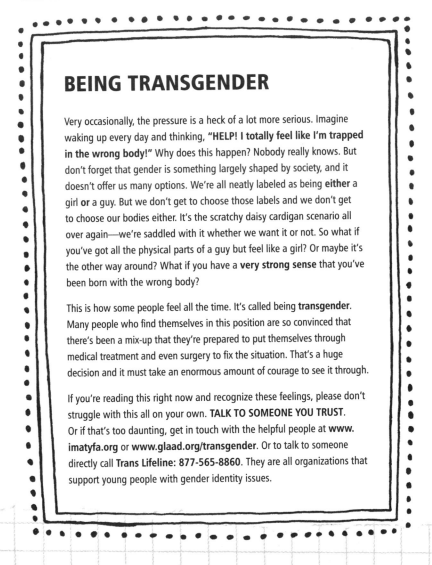

BEING TRANSGENDER

Very occasionally, the pressure is a heck of a lot more serious. Imagine waking up every day and thinking, **"HELP! I totally feel like I'm trapped in the wrong body!"** Why does this happen? Nobody really knows. But don't forget that gender is something largely shaped by society, and it doesn't offer us many options. We're all neatly labeled as being **either** a girl **or** a guy. But we don't get to choose those labels and we don't get to choose our bodies either. It's the scratchy daisy cardigan scenario all over again—we're saddled with it whether we want it or not. So what if you've got all the physical parts of a guy but feel like a girl? Or maybe it's the other way around? What if you have a **very strong sense** that you've been born with the wrong body?

This is how some people feel all the time. It's called being **transgender**. Many people who find themselves in this position are so convinced that there's been a mix-up that they're prepared to put themselves through medical treatment and even surgery to fix the situation. That's a huge decision and it must take an enormous amount of courage to see it through.

If you're reading this right now and recognize these feelings, please don't struggle with this all on your own. **TALK TO SOMEONE YOU TRUST**. Or if that's too daunting, get in touch with the helpful people at **www. imatyfa.org** or **www.glaad.org/transgender**. Or to talk to someone directly call **Trans Lifeline: 877-565-8860**. They are all organizations that support young people with gender identity issues.

But for the vast majority of us, the pressure is much closer to something like this:

And before we know it, we're **judging** ourselves—and perhaps we're judging other people too. Like this:

Are you any good at being a girl?

Check the box if you . . .

- ☐ love the color pink
- ☐ look hot in spaghetti straps
- ☐ can walk effortlessly in very high heels
- ☐ have long and lustrous* hair
- ☐ can apply eyeliner with one hand
- ☐ feel like the talk of the town on Valentine's Day

But—as always—judging how **good** you are at being a girl is not this simple. Having said that, if you scored six out of six, that's great! Straighten up your spaghetti straps, flick back your lustrous hair, and keep on doing your thing **just the way you are**. There's **definitely nothing wrong** with being the type of girl that society would love us all to be. It's just useful to remember this:

OTHER MODELS ARE AVAILABLE.

---

* I've read this word a billion times on shampoo bottles. I just looked it up. It means splendid, brilliant, and shiny.

Girls and boys **aren't** made out of gingerbread and we haven't all been cut into shape with a cookie cutter. **It doesn't matter** if we don't look like the people in the films and on the commercials and it doesn't matter if we don't really identify with them either. The truth is that **we're all different**. And some boys like pink and some girls like football and some people have upturned noses and some thirteen-year-old girls still don't need bras. **Right** and **wrong** doesn't even come into it.*

So if you didn't score six, or if you didn't score any, that's great too! Because there are a thousand ways of being a girl. Your own unique way is one of them.

---

* Just so long as we try to be halfway decent human beings. No one likes a jerk.

The gender power imbalance

As much as my fingers want to fall off as I type this, it wouldn't be right for anyone to write a book called *Being a Girl* without pointing out this one

horrible,
UNAVOIDABLE
fact.

It's a man's world.

I've said it quietly to try to make it less traumatic to read. But there it is. The reality. Oceans are wet and deserts are dry and we are girls living in a world dominated by men.

It's not fair, I know. In fact, if you think about it too hard, it will make your blood boil. Because it's not our fault. Then again, please don't start hating every male on the planet, because it's not their fault either.

It's just how it is. For now.

This has been the situation for a **very** long time. I suppose it's another odd souvenir from way, **way** back, when we all still lived in caves. Being able to hunt wild animals and cart home heavy chunks of meat to feed the family was absolutely essential—because supermarkets and corner stores hadn't been invented yet. But somebody also had to stay in the cave and look after the babies—because daycares didn't exist yet either. So men went out to kill the beasties and bring back the meat, and women stayed in the cave. These became their **gender roles**. It also meant that while the women spent every second of the day taking care of the kids, the men got to take care of everything else. This gave them power. Power in the hands of the wrong cavemen created unequal societies. All these millennia later (and despite many improvements), men still have more opportunities to stamp their opinions all over the world than women do. This is known as . . .

Societies can take a long time to change.

Let's just pause here. I need you to read the following words out loud. It's important.

It's nice to like boys.
They didn't ask for this gender power imbalance any more than we did.

Maybe you're thinking, *Yeah, but what do power-crazy random cavemen have to do with anything? The world has moved on.*

Well, yes, it has. But only quite recently. Think about it. How many massively famous men can you name from **way back**?

Well, for starters, there's:

> Leonardo da Vinci, Julius Caesar, William Shakespeare, Captain James Cook, Christopher Columbus, Mark Twain, Abraham Lincoln, Ludwig van Beethoven, the Prophet Muhammad, Thomas Jefferson, Sir Isaac Newton, William Wordsworth, Charles Dickens, Wolfgang Amadeus Mozart, Napoleon Bonaparte, Paul Revere, Jesus, Myles Standish, Sir Arthur Conan Doyle, Attila the Hun, Vlad the Impaler, George Washington, J.R.R. Tolkien, Marco Polo, Alfred the . . .

I could go on.

But try making a list of massively famous women who lived centuries ago and it's a lot more difficult.

> Elizabeth I, Queen Victoria, Charlotte, Anne, and Emily Brontë, Anne Boleyn, Marie Antoinette, Pocahontas . . . um . . .

And that's a seriously unsatisfactory list because Elizabeth and Victoria only became queens because they didn't have brothers who could run the country instead of them. And Charlotte, Anne, and Emily Brontë first published their books under the names Currer, Acton, and Ellis Bell so that their readers wouldn't know they were reading the words of women. And Anne Boleyn and Marie Antoinette are mostly known for being married to kings and getting their heads chopped off. And Pocahontas was doing just fine in her Native American tribe when she was kidnapped by English settlers who thought that they knew better.

Of course, there **are** other famous women who could be added to the list but not nearly so many as there should be. And it's not because women weren't ever interesting in the olden days; it's just that they didn't often get a chance to have their stories heard or recorded. History really is **his** story. For a long time, it was written pretty much exclusively **by** men **about** men.

If all this is starting to upset you, I need you to take a big, deep breath and say some more words out loud:

Boys are necessary and good for our future existence.

Got that?

OK, let's continue.

The suffragettes

Fortunately, things are changing. Since World War I, the gender power imbalance has leveled out a bit. And that's got a lot to do with a group of women known as **the suffragettes**. These women were feminists.* They lived in the late 1800s and early 1900s and campaigned very actively and courageously for the right of women to vote. Yes, believe it or not, before then women—that is, half the population—did <u>not</u> have the right to vote!

In the United States, one of the most active campaigners was **Elizabeth Cady Stanton** (1815–1902). As well as saying that women should have the right to vote, Elizabeth said some other important things too. She said that women should be given the same opportunities in education and in the workplace as men, and that any woman should have the right to ask for a divorce or for birth control if that was what she wanted. Oh, and Elizabeth also made it very clear that nobody should ever try to stop a woman from putting on her bloomers and riding a bicycle. Hooray for the good sense of Elizabeth Cady Stanton! Thanks to her and to other similarly outspoken women around the world, most countries now allow women to vote.

So when you're older and all the politicians are spouting garbage and you feel you can't really be bothered to drag yourself to the voting booth, do it anyway. Elizabeth would be proud of you.

Hurrah!

---

* A feminist is someone who believes in equality of the sexes.

But hey, wake up, grandma! This is the twenty-first century!

Yes it is. But the struggle for equality isn't over yet.

~~~~~~~~~~~~~~~~~~~~~~~~~~~~

Sexism

There's still a lot of shady sexism sloshing around. Did you know that the average man still earns a lot more than the average woman? Currently, in the United States, female full-time workers make about 79 cents for every dollar earned by men.

One area where this pay gap is very public and very obvious is sports. In 2015, the average salary for a player in the men's professional soccer league (MLS) was estimated to be $226,455.* In the equivalent women's league (NWSL), pay is capped so that no player can earn more than $39,700 (not even ⅕ of the average male player), and most are paid far less.

Surely that's a foul!

In case you hadn't noticed, American girls are extremely good at soccer. In July 2015, the United States beat Japan in the final match of the FIFA Women's World Cup. The score was 5–2 and three of those winning goals were scored by the US captain, Carli Lloyd. Carli was also the 2015 FIFA World Player of the Year. Go, Carli!

- -

* That pay data can be found at www.americansocceranalysis.com.

Everyday Sexism

You may have heard of this phrase. That's because it's being used as a meme to expose everyday sexual prejudice and inequality. This simple idea allows women all over the world to speak out about the gripes, annoyances, and sometimes totally unfair treatment they experience on a daily basis. One woman tweeted that she wasn't allowed to rent a motorboat while she was on vacation. The reason? She was a woman and therefore "more likely to crash!" Another woman said she'd been told to eat more because "men like something to squeeze." Someone else was told she was too obsessed with her job because she wasn't married and didn't have kids.

As of June 2016, @EverydaySexism has around 250,000 followers on Twitter. I'm not sure whether this tells us something exciting or depressing. But it certainly says that women aren't prepared to let sexist behavior pass for normal any more. You can find out more about the Everyday Sexism campaign at **www.everydaysexism.com**.

It's not just about people's actions, I'm afraid. Sexism is **everywhere**. Even in the words we speak. In college, you study to become a **Bachelor** of Arts.* Or a **Bachelor** of Science. If you study a bit more, you can become a **Master** of Arts or Science. And anything that's never been pulled out of the ground, or never grown on a plant, or never breathed or burped or blinked, is described as being **man**-made.

---

* A bachelor is an unmarried man. Four years of hard work in college and this is what you become. How weird is that? Admittedly, it sounds better than Spinster of the Arts. A spinster is an unmarried woman. Something about the word spinster just sounds totally tragic.

You've probably noticed an outrageously unfair language situation at school too. You know that girl who's had a few boyfriends? Yep. You know the one. That girl who gets called slut, bimbo, floozy, skank, ho, hussy, hooker, and tramp?

Now think about Randy Studman—that boy who can't keep it in his pants. What does he get called?

* PLAYER *

Yes, girlfriends—life's a <u>**bitch**</u>. Yup. There is a reason your parents probably don't want you using the term "bitch." Because it's seriously nasty toward women. See page 35. The best thing we can do is **rise right above it** and shove the sexist name-calling in the trash. Oops.

Here come the girls

This chapter is going to end very soon, but I really don't want you to go away feeling depressed. Or disappointed. Or cheated. Or foot-stompingly furious. And I certainly don't want you to storm over to your brother / boyfriend / dad / uncle / guy-friend and start giving him a hard time. So let's feel positive and strong and think about the good stuff. Most people today—female **and** male—are doing all they can to turn that gender power imbalance into much more of an evenly matched seesaw.

And I'm going to pitch in right now by taking this opportunity to name-check just a few of the many brilliant women who seem to have been swallowed up by history.

SEVEN WOMEN TO REMEMBER

ADA *Lovelace*

Just because she has the best name, let's start with **Ada Lovelace** (1815–1852). She was an English mathematician who is often described as the world's first computer programmer. Even so, for many people, the most memorable detail about her is that she was the daughter of the famous Romantic poet Lord Byron. The truth is that Ada Lovelace really didn't need a famous dad to be interesting— she was an extraordinary person anyway. By the time she was twelve, Ada had carried out her own scientific studies on the principles of flight and written up her conclusions in a book she called *Flyology*. It is hardly any wonder that she grew up to be one of the first-ever computer programmer whiz kids. Happily, the world is slowly waking up to the importance of Ada's contributions to science, technology, engineering, and mathematics. There is now even an Ada Lovelace Day. Look out for it next October.

MARY Seacole

You may have heard of Florence Nightingale (1820–1910), but have you heard of **Mary Seacole**? She was a Jamaican-born British woman who lived from 1805 to 1881. Like Florence Nightingale, Mary was a nurse who looked after soldiers during the Crimean War. She even set up her own hospital to look after them. The injured soldiers liked Mary so much that they nicknamed her "Mother Seacole." Good work, Mary!

MARY Edwards Walker

Another woman who risked everything to help others during wartime was **Mary Edwards Walker** (1832–1919). In spite of the limited opportunities offered to women at that time, Mary went to college and qualified as a surgeon. At the outbreak of the American Civil War, she quickly volunteered to work as a surgeon for the Union Army. However, Mary didn't want to treat only wounded soldiers, she also wanted to help wounded civilians—even if that meant crossing over enemy lines. Unfortunately, this led to Mary being captured by the Confederate army and arrested as a spy, but eventually she was released unharmed. After the war, Mary was arrested several more times for the extraordinary crime of "wearing men's clothes." In response to this, Mary said, "I don't wear men's clothes, I wear my own clothes." Very well said, Mary.

SYBIL *Ludington*

Have you heard about how Paul Revere (1734–1818) rode his horse eighteen miles to warn the rebel militia of approaching British troops at the outbreak of the American Revolutionary War? Then maybe you've also heard about **Sybil Ludington** (1761–1839)? She also jumped on her horse and rode through the night to alert the rebels. The only difference is that she rode approximately forty miles and she was only sixteen years old at the time. That makes her at least twice as heroic as Paul Revere!

Another real **shero** is **Harriet Tubman** (c.1820–1913). An African-American, she was born into slavery but at age twenty-nine she escaped. You'd think she would put her feet up after that, wouldn't you? Get herself a nice little place by the sea and take things easy. Not Harriet. She had unfinished business. Risking her life, she returned many times to the American slave states

HARRIET *Tubman*

and guided more than three hundred other slaves to freedom via a network of **safe houses** known as the Underground Railroad. Harriet Tubman is famous for saying, "I never lost a passenger."

In 2016 the U.S. Department of the Treasury announced that Harriett Tubman will be the new face of the twenty-dollar bill, making her both the first woman and the only African American given this honor in modern-day paper currency. This important recognition is well overdue and very welcome!

If you don't know that Neil Armstrong was the first man to walk on the moon, there's a good chance you live on the moon. But do you know who the first woman in space was? No? Well, it was a Russian cosmonaut—**astronaut,** if you prefer—called **Valentina Tereshkova** (born in 1937). Valentina went into space on June 16, 1963, in a spacecraft called *Vostok 6.* So now you know.

VALENTINA Tereshkova

HEDY Lamarr

Last, but not least, I'm going to end this list of sheroes with **Hedy Lamarr** (1914–2000). As well as being ridiculously clever, Hedy Lamarr was also ridiculously beautiful. She had it all. She was a big movie star in the Golden Age of Hollywood who also happened to invent a "secret communications system." Apart from being a useful wartime gadget, this also formed the basis of that handy thingamajig we use all the time today called "Wi-Fi."

All those women are part of **herstory**. But plenty more women are stamping their mark on today's world. Here are a few of them.

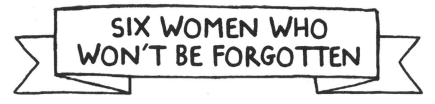

SIX WOMEN WHO WON'T BE FORGOTTEN

Any list of incredible modern women would be totally remiss if it didn't include **Malala Yousafzai**. At age fifteen, Malala was shot by Taliban gunmen just because she wanted to go to school. Incredibly, she survived and campaigned *LOUDER THAN EVER* for the rights of girls to be educated. In 2014, at only seventeen years old, Malala became the youngest ever person to receive the Nobel Peace Prize. This teen girl must be one of the strongest and bravest human beings in the world.

Someone else with a big helping of "girl power" is **Angela Merkel**. She's the Chancellor of Germany—equivalent to the president—and that makes her a very powerful and important person indeed!

Then we've got pop megastars like **Beyoncé** and **Adele**. They're both so famous they don't even need last names. But the **best thing** about this feisty duo is not their fame or their billion-selling records or their bling—it's the fact that they are **blatantly in charge** of everything they do. No one would dare boss **them** around.

Women are owning the book world too. If you Google "bestselling teen books," chances are two names will crop up more than any others: **J.K. Rowling** and **Suzanne Collins**. Once upon a time, lots of people believed that boys wouldn't want to read books that were written by women.* I think these two have totally disproved that notion.

---

* That might be why Joanne Kathleen Rowling chose to use her initials instead of her name. Then again, maybe she just thought J.K. sounded better. In which case, why not? After all, they're her initials. She can use them however she wants.

So where does all this leave you?

That's where.

It may still be a bit of a man's world, but the future is smelling sweeter than ever.

You are a girl of today and a woman of tomorrow.

The future is yours. Seize it with both hands.

For more information on sheroes past, present, and future, check out these awesome sites:

National Women's History Museum (www.nwhm.org)

SheHeroes (www.sheheroes.org)

Chapter 3

ALLEY CATS & ADOLESCENCE

We've got the whole world in our hands. So why are so many of us girls still feeling stressed?

. . . from the ads and from TV and from films and from boys and from your parents and from the internet and from random passersby in the street and from pretty much **every-flipping-thing.**

But not from other girls, right?

Because we're all in this **girl sitch** together and the last thing we'd do is make life worse for ourselves, right?

Surely we are a **united sisterhood** and we support each other past the sexism and pimples and the periods, **and are totally nice to each other.** *Right?*

Here comes the trickiest headache of all:

GIRLS AREN'T ALWAYS NICE TO EACH OTHER.

Or, as one of the girls in my Student Focus Group puts it:

other girls are bitches

Although actually, the word "**bitch**" is a little misleading. Because a bitch is a female dog. And what do dogs do? They pee on fire hydrants, chase Frisbees, and bark at mailmen. Doesn't sound much like girls, does it?

In fact, girls have much more in common with cats. Cats are clever. They're smooth operators. No one should ever assume that all they do is flounce about and look nice. Annoy a cat at your own risk—because even the sweetest and prettiest one has claws. Put two fiesty cats together in a confined space and you could find yourself staring at a scene of **carnage**. Because cats—and girls—unfortunately have the capacity to be vicious. What seems to be a perfectly reasonable creature one moment might well morph into a hissing **alley cat** the next.

Enter the jungle

Nowhere is the cattiness of girls more evident than in middle school. It is like a wild jungle. And sometimes it feels as if throwing a hissy fit and getting your claws out is the only way to stay alive.

Maybe.

But perhaps it's smarter just to use your brain and avoid the most vicious circles. And it's easier to do this if you know exactly who you're dealing with. Take a close look at the table on the next page:

THE ORDER OF CATS

QUEEN CAT

Often fairly fancy to look at, these feline specimens are the pack leaders. Highly territorial, they mark out their boundaries by rubbing their scent around. Once this is done, they **rule the joint.** Most likely to be found hanging around their own cat trees.

CLIQUE CATS

Otherwise known as **the pack.** Individually they're often unimpressive, but, combined, they can be a **terrifying force.** Every clique cat **worships** and **fears** her queen cat in more-or-less equal doses. They flock around her and constantly jostle for a higher position within the pack. The queen cat will pick and choose favorites from among them. And then drop them like a bag of garbage.

COPY CATS

These cats all look the same. That's because they curl up in front of the TV every night and pay very close attention to what all the celebrity glamour pusses look like. Then they copy them. Also known as the **identi-cats.**

THE MOTLEY CREW

Most cats fall into this category. But that doesn't mean they're uninteresting—because each member of the motley crew is different. Some are scrawny. Some are chubby. Some are fast. Some are slow. Some are sweet. Some aren't. The one thing they all share is a lack of confidence.

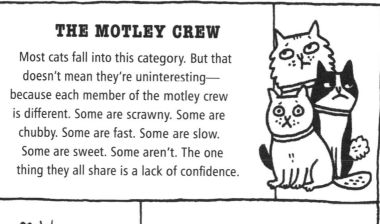

THE WANDERING STRAY

The one whose name nobody can remember. Floats between cats and doesn't really bond with any of them. Of course, if there are lots of clique cats about, who can blame her?

CAT FOOD

Frightened little things who keep their heads down and try to be invisible. Also known as mice.

THE LIONESS

There's another type of cat who's not on this table. That's because she doesn't belong on it. She's in a **league of her own**. This creature is the **lioness**. And any cat who has any sense respects her. In fact, any *boy* who has any sense respects her too.

So what's the lioness got that's so hot?

CONFIDENCE

Yep. It's as simple as that. But it's the one thing that all those other cats don't have.

Having an air of confidence is like wearing the best-smelling perfume in the world.

Now be careful, here—I'm not talking about **in-your-face** attitude. Or arrogance. Those things stink of budget air freshener.

I'm talking about **quiet inner strength**—the type that keeps your head held high and stops you from making a sad mewing noise whenever you open your mouth. No lioness needs to stomp around with a clique to feel important. And she doesn't need fake fur to feel beautiful. She just is, anyway. **Truly beautiful.** The sort of beautiful that starts from **inside** and shows itself to the world in the form of a genuine smile.

OK, so lions don't actually smile. But think how **beyond totally amazing** they'd look if they did. Anyway, I think you get my gist:

confidence + kindness earns respect from others.

Or if that sounds too cheesy, try thinking of it this way instead:

Look people in the eye and be nice to them.

They will respect you for it.

Honestly, it works.

But, I know, when you're thirteen and still flat-chested, feeling confident is a whole lot easier said than done. So, keep calm and contemplate these five points:

1. Queen cats aren't actually all that confident either. That's why you hardly ever see them on their own.

2. Everyone has unsure moments at school—and everywhere else. Even lionesses.

3. You're awesome, aren't you? **YES**, you are. There's no one else like you in the whole world. That's a **fact**. You're a limited edition of one. Even if you're an identical twin.

4. Bras come in **all** shapes and sizes—including flat and small.

5. Pimples don't last forever. Neither does school.

And that brings us nicely to the next question.

Why are middle school and high school such catty places?

If I knew the answer to that I'd be Yoda.
But my guess is that it's got a lot to do with

HORMONES.

Because there you all are in first grade—all happy little girls together and playing with your Barbie dolls and action figures. Life is fairly straightforward. But then you get a bit older and **weird things start to happen**. For some girls, these **weird things** might begin while they are still only seven or eight—but for most, the **weirdness** begins in middle school.

~~~~~~~~~~~~~~~~~~~~~~~~~~~~~

Adolescence and puberty

Yes. **Operation Puberty has begun.**

But why?

Think of it like this:

Your brain wants a new outfit. It's been wearing the same body for about twelve years and it's feeling uncool. But there's no way that a **brain** can walk into Hollister or H&M and start scanning the racks for this season's latest body—so it has to do something more drastic. It starts releasing **weird chemicals** into your bloodstream. These **weird chemicals** are called hormones and they are going to turn you into an **adult**.

Obviously this is a **seriously major project**. An extreme makeover like this can't just happen overnight. It's going to take years. Probably until you're about fifteen or sixteen. Maybe even later. And during these years of physical change—**puberty**—you're going to have a fair amount of temporary inconvenience. And sometimes, the whole thing might get on your nerves a bit and make you ever so slightly

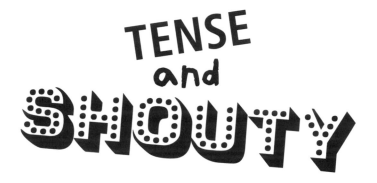

AND THINGS WOULDN'T BE HALF AS BAD IF PEOPLE DIDN'T KEEP MAKING A FUSS ABOUT IT!

Let's call this whole experience—physical and emotional—**adolescence**. Because, quite frankly, adolescence is a much more pleasant-sounding word than

pyoooberty.

What's happening to you is **normal**. And it happens to everyone. Of course, you know this already. But it's very easy to forget it with all those hormones freaking you out. Perhaps this explains why some girls are a bit high-strung in middle school and high school.

The changes

If you haven't yet heard about them in a special health class or video, you probably will. But let's go through each of the changes anyway.

Your hair. It's going to grow. And not just on your head. It's going to start sprouting under your armpits and on your legs and downstairs in the underwear department. You may find that you're a bit hairier in other places too. Don't worry. This is all perfectly normal. Hair is a **big** subject. We'll discuss it in-depth later on.

Your face. It's going to change a bit. It may get longer and your cheekbones and jaw may take on a more defined shape. But this will happen so subtly you probably won't even notice. In fact, the only noticeable thing is the havoc these changes might wreak on your skin.

For a while, your face may look shiny and feel a little greasy. You may see that you're getting pimples popping up overnight. And if you get really close to the mirror and stare at yourself so hard that you go cross-eyed, you may also see lots of little black dots covering your nose, chin, and forehead. These are **blackheads**. <u>**Pimples and blackheads have got nothing to do with dirt.**</u> They're just another stressful inconvenience of adolescence. Because of all the weirdness created by your raging hormones, your skin has gone bonkers and started producing way too much oil. Trying to fix the situation is a bit like playing that game *Whack-a-Mole*. Well, that's how it is with pimples too. Think of it as *Whack-a-Zit*. You squeeze one and three more pop up in its place.

Don't squeeze them—you could get scars and these are even worse than pimples because they stick around forever.

As tempting as it may be to plaster your face in foundation, that's not going to help either—**because putting more stuff on clogged pores is only going to block them more.** See Diagram One:

Diagram One: The Vicious Circle

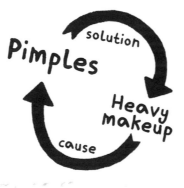

It's much better just to wash your face with a mild soap twice a day and avoid using oily makeup. But if the pimple situation gets so bad that you want to scream, go to the dermatologist for some advice. There are treatments that can help.

And remember—most of your peers are playing *Whack-a-Zit* as well. In theory, this shouldn't make you feel any better. In reality, it probably does.

Your breasts. If you don't have them yet, you soon will. This is actually the **weirdest**—but perhaps the best—part of the whole female adolescent experience. And unlike the changing shape of your face, this is **not** subtle at all. First of all, your **areola**—that's that dark circle around your nipple*—is going to go a bit puffy. At this stage, you may feel like you need to get yourself something called a **training bra**. You may feel like doing this anyway—puffiness or not. In which case, memorize the following words by heart and say them nicely to your mom.

I can 99.9 percent guarantee that you'll have a bra by the end of the week.

---

* One of these is an areola. Two or more are called areolae. This is way too complicated. Let's just deal with one areola at a time.

The next thing you'll notice is the development of **breast buds**—a visible bump under each nipple. Basically it will look as if Mother Nature is inflating your bazookas with a bicycle pump. (By the way, *NEVER EVER* say breast buds out loud. Everyone within a five-mile radius will instantly collapse with a cringe attack.) Your BBs will continue growing until they've reached their adult shape.

Brand new pair of boobs.

How **utterly** amazing is that?

Oh, but there's one more thing you should know about them. Each boob will do its own thing. They won't necessarily develop at the same pace, so you could be a bit uneven for a while. And there isn't actually any guarantee that they'll ever match up exactly. This is very normal. A pair of breasts is rarely totally symmetrical.

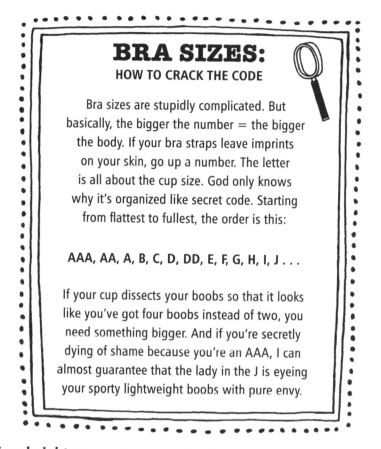

BRA SIZES:
HOW TO CRACK THE CODE

Bra sizes are stupidly complicated. But basically, the bigger the number = the bigger the body. If your bra straps leave imprints on your skin, go up a number. The letter is all about the cup size. God only knows why it's organized like secret code. Starting from flattest to fullest, the order is this:

AAA, AA, A, B, C, D, DD, E, F, G, H, I, J . . .

If your cup dissects your boobs so that it looks like you've got four boobs instead of two, you need something bigger. And if you're secretly dying of shame because you're an AAA, I can almost guarantee that the lady in the J is eyeing your sporty lightweight boobs with pure envy.

Your height. You're going to get taller.* Between the ages of ten and sixteen, it's normal to grow three inches a year. That might not sound like much but, trust me, **it is**. Your body is going to need **food**. Try to give it some top quality nourishment—vegetables and fruit– rather than cramming your mouth full of Fritos and gummy bears. Chips and candy are tasty as an occasional treat but they don't contain the vital things your growing body needs on its journey to becoming a healthy adult—i.e. vitamins, minerals, protein, and fiber.

---

* How much taller will vary from person to person. Obviously. As much as we might long to strut around on legs that come up to our armpits, Mother Nature may have other plans. I know this for a fact because I never made it past five feet and half an inch. But you know that saying—good things come in little packages? Yeah, well, IT'S TRUE.

Periods. These will start. You may wish they hadn't. Let's be respectful and give them a whole chapter of their own. (That's the next chapter, so be prepared.)

All this is stuff you've probably been expecting anyway. But there's a couple of other developments that you won't necessarily be aware of. You need to know about them.

BRACE YOURSELF FOR
A SERIOUS ANNOUNCEMENT

Your vagina. Hoo-ha. Koochie. Lady bits. Vajayjay. Whatever. It's going through some changes too. You may sometimes find a clear white discharge in your undies. **This is OK. You're not dying.** It's just nature's way of keeping grown-up you clean. Panic over.

AND ANOTHER ONE

Sweat glands. You can't see them but they'll be there. Sweaty areas around your armpits, breasts, and crotch.

It may feel weird at first but everyone else deals with it. Just keep yourself washed and clean and use an underarm deodorant daily. I'm telling you this because I am your friend.

So there we have it. Changing you from a girl into a young woman is a **crazy complicated business**. Some days you might be feeling thoroughly annoyed with the whole process and just want to hibernate in bed. But instead, you've got to go to school—that place where you're forced to suffer the horror of . . .

The gym locker room

You know what I'm talking about.

A great big gaggle of girls all slyly checking each other out to see who has boobs and who doesn't. Who's shaving her legs and who isn't. Who's stuck up about being a 36D and who's still in a training bra. You'll look back and laugh about it one day, but, right now, it might feel like a **really unfunny joke**.

Try not to be bothered by anyone else's buxom boobs or gazelle-length legs. All girls are different. Some are practically full-grown by the age of twelve and some are only just getting going then. **Everyone develops at different speeds**. Just because your magic makeover hormones haven't kicked in yet doesn't mean they won't. They will. And if, after reading this, you're **still** not convinced and are seriously worried that something is wrong, try talking to someone older. Like your mom or your sister or your cool aunt or your pediatrician. **No one** wants you to be stressing about this.

The other thing to keep in mind is that **everyone else** in the gym locker room is probably feeling just as self-conscious as you are. Because nobody ever really likes a communal changing room. That's why half-decent shops and swimming pools have the good sense to offer individual stalls. And if anybody ever says to you:

> Ooooh . . .
> My favorite memory of high school is definitely getting changed for PE in front of all my classmates!

. . . they're either:

a.) lying
    or
b.) insane
    or
c.) both.

Still feeling the pressure?

Well, you won't be on your own. Because you know all those other girls in your class? The queen and the clique cats and the strays and the motleys and the cat food? Some days they feel stressed and totally overwhelmed too.

When you take everything into consideration, it's no wonder that . . .

other girls are bitches

. . . sometimes.

If boys had periods and breast buds and vaginal discharge to deal with, they'd probably be bitches too. Weathering the odd catty comment is part of growing up. That bitchy remark says a lot more about the person who's made it than it **ever** does about anyone else. It says that they're having a bad-tempered, stressed-out, insecure, and thoughtless moment. Distance yourself and leave them to it. Most of us have regrettable moments like that occasionally.

BUT

. . . and it's a very big but . . .

Having hormones whizzing around in your body is no excuse for behaving like

a

TOTAL

JERK.

And that brings us to a colossally unfunny subject.

Bullying

Repeatedly picking on someone and making them feel bad <u>is</u> BULLYING. It's NOT fooling around. It's NOT a joke. And it's NOT OK.

In fact, it's awful.

On or off the internet.

So if you ever find yourself caught up with the crowd and behaving like a clique cat—just have a bit of class and dignity and stop it **immediately**. Thank you.

And if it's happening to you or someone you know—**don't let it continue.** Take positive, lion-sized steps to end it.

HOW TO BEAT THE BULLIES

Make it clear you are NOT cat food. Bullies may seem as hard as nails but actually they're stinking cowards. Pretty often, it just takes a little sign of inner strength from you to make them crawl back under their rocks.

If this doesn't work, keep a written list of every mean thing that's been said or done to you and make a note of the dates too. This is evidence. You must not let this awfulness go unchallenged.

Show your evidence to a teacher you trust. It doesn't matter whether that teacher knows the bully (or bullies) or not. By telling someone who has **a duty of care** to you, you are no longer on your own with this problem. This is not snitching. This is not tattling. This is not ratting anyone out. It is putting a stop to an inexcusable situation. They must not be allowed to keep doing this.

Ultimately, you need to

LET YOUR INNER LIONESS

roar!

WARNING: this page is dark.

Unfortunately, bullying has mutated with the times. It's gone digital.
Forget school, these days it's **the internet** where girls can really ruin each
other's lives. **And in a way, this is as low-down and shady as bullying
gets.** Because if you're unlucky enough to be on the receiving end of
cyberbullying, it can feel like the nastiness is endless and everywhere.

Trolls are called trolls for a reason. They're pathetic and charmless
monsters who hide in shady dark places. And they are **NOT** to be trusted.

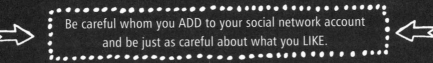

Be careful whom you ADD to your social network account
and be just as careful about what you LIKE.

If you suspect a comment is sketchy, run it past this simple **Troll Test**:

WOULD I BE OK WITH THAT
IF IT WAS SAID ABOUT ME?

If the answer is **NO**, steer clear of the person who made the comment.
REPORT their comment if you can. **UNFRIEND** them if you can.**WHATEVER**
you do, **DON'T GET INVOLVED** with this conversation or thread.

And if that nasty comment is about YOU—**DON'T RESPOND**.
BLOCK the troll who made it and
TALK TO A TEACHER OR ANOTHER ADULT YOU TRUST.

This sad troll needs to learn that **CYBERBULLYING IS NOT OK.**
By taking a couple of simple steps, you are actually helping her (or him)
learn to be nicer.

Unfortunately, the truth is, it's not just bullies who heap the pressure on. Sometimes **friends** do it to each other. This is known as . . .

Peer pressure

It's a weird thing but that yucky sensation of feeling threatened isn't always caused by the people we think of as bullies. Sometimes— especially when you're a teenager—you can get that same gut-sinking feeling from your very own "friends."

Ever heard something like this?

No offense but you're a drag sometimes.*

Come on! Stop being so lame.

Don't be so boring.

Or maybe it's **YOU** who's waved a cigarette in your best friend's face and said:

How do you know you don't like it if you won't even try it?

* No offense but if you ever catch yourself starting a statement with this phrase just stop immediately. Because there's a good chance you're about to say something seriously offensive. You should also stop everything if you start a sentence with any of these: *Not to be mean . . . Not to be racist . . . Not to be homophobic . . .*

It may seem harmless, but if this kind of thing happens a lot, it can start to feel like bullying—even though nothing much was ever meant by it and you're all supposed to be friends.

The bottom line is this: **nobody should ever be making you do stuff that you're not comfortable with.**

And obviously, that works the other way around too. You shouldn't be pestering your reluctant friend into getting a tattoo.

Cigarettes, booze, and drugs

OK—maybe I made it sound too cut-and-dried back there.

We **all** have to do **some** things we're not happy about—like exams and chores and going to the dentist. These things are a pain in the butt but they're good for us. But smoking and drinking and taking non-prescription drugs aren't **ever** good for us. Also, unless you're eighteen, smoking is actually illegal so you're **breaking the law** anyway. And unless you're over twenty-one, you're breaking the law drinking alcohol too. And taking—or even possessing—any other kind of illegal drug is a **criminal offense at any age**. Aside from this, the wise lionesses among us will have noticed that smoking cigarettes and getting drunk or high or stoned isn't even cool.

There is NOTHING attractive
about reeking like an ashtray.

And anyone who says that they **prefer** to kiss someone who tastes like an ashtray is either—yep, you guessed it . . .

a.) lying
  or
b.) insane
  or
c.) both.

There are even better reasons not to smoke though. For one, smoking means you're much more likely to end up with gross teeth, yellow fingers, thin hair, a wrinkly face, and a puckered-up mouth, and for another thing, you're much more likely to wind up with cancer.

Knocking back alcohol until you puke isn't sexy or cool either. It's **not** cool to be unsafe. If you ever see a girl staggering around with a bottle in her hand and her dress caught up in her underwear, you can be quite sure you are seeing a girl who needs a bit of assistance from her friends. And probably a taxi home to her parents.

Then there's the other stuff. I hate to sound like a total prude but drugs aren't cool either. People who are high will often think they're **incredibly interesting** and will feel the need to talk about how **incredibly interesting** they are for an **incredibly long time**. Even when there's no one listening.

And rolling up a scruffy little joint full of grass or weed or skunk or Mary Jane* and getting stoned isn't cool either. In fact, you'll be competing to find out who wins the title of Most Boring Person in the World. Because it turns you into someone who can't even be bothered to

finish what. . .

So if you don't care for any of these tempting propositions, it definitely doesn't mean you're a loser. It actually means that you've got your head screwed on right.

If you want to do your own research, a good place to start is **teens.drugabuse.gov**. There are also other useful resources at the back of this book.

* Call it what you like—the real names for this stuff are cannabis and marijuana.

Saying no

Putting a lid on peer pressure is all about **confidence** again. It's about having the courage to **be who you want to be.** Your cig-puffing friends may think they look cooler than the coolest people on Planet Cool—but they don't even know what cool **is** until they've seen you give them a shrug and say:

No, thanks. I'll pass.

And if they have any kind of issue with that and give you a hard time, then—as disappointing as it might be—there's only one thing left to do.

DITCH THEM LIKE A BAG OF GARBAGE.

What to do if you think YOU'VE been an alley cat

If reading any of this has made your cheeks burn, it's not the end of the world. The truth is that most of us could do with being nicer to the people around us. It's just that sometimes we forget. The important thing is to recognize when you've been a bit mean and to put things right. It's not hard to do, actually. Just **stop** doing or saying whatever it is that might not be that kind. And if you really think or know that you've made someone feel awful, there's only one word that can make things better.

Just that. Not:

Or:

Or:

The last three aren't so much apologies as **nonpologies**. No one cares two hoots about a nonpology. Just say **sorry**. It can be surprisingly hard to get out sometimes but it's the only word that actually works.

A QUICK WORD
ABOUT YOUR 'RENTS

Your adolescence puts pressure on them too. Parents, grandparents, guardians—whoever they are, they'll want to help. But there's only so much they can do. And they think they know their sweet little girl—but sometimes, instead of her, they see a snarling alley cat who's ready to pounce.

You know the one I mean? She's got an attitude as big as Texas and a face like a sour lemon.

Give your adults a break and try not to give them such a hard time. They're getting old and tired. And you live in their house, monopolize their TV, and gobble up all their grub. They deserve a bit of your patience and understanding. After all, one day you may have a snarling alley cat of your own to deal with.

 Ooof. It's probably time to lighten up a little. Cast your mind back to Chapter 1, when I promised you I had . . .

Inside information about what boys think

It's time to share some of it with you. I asked the boys in my Student Focus Group what kind of girls they liked. This is what they said:

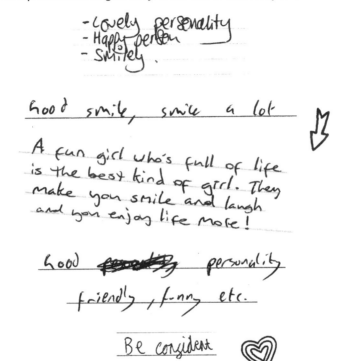

- Lovely personality
- Happy person
- Smiley.

Good smile, smile a lot

A fun girl who's full of life is the best kind of girl. They make you smile and laugh and you enjoy life more!

Good ~~personality~~ personality friendly, funny etc.

Be confident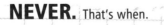

Whether you're into boys or not, this all sounds like a good image to be aiming for. Since when has anyone ever said, **"Oh I hate being known as that confident, happy, smiley, friendly, fun girl with the great personality?"**

NEVER. That's when.

Before we move on . . .

I want you to remember that it's not all pimples and peer pressure.

When girls are being nice to each other, they totally rock. Teenage girls do the friend thing better than anyone else.

Those girls you're friends with now are people you're likely to remember forever. Maybe you'll even know them forever too, and, one day, you'll be heading out to bingo night with **[INSERT YOUR FRIEND'S NAME HERE]** and chatting to each other about your grandchildren.

After all, that's what a BFF is all about, isn't it?

School does feel like a major drag sometimes. And so does adolescence. But with a smile on your face and a few sweet comments to the people who see you every day, you can help make planet Earth a less catty place. And that, my friend, is called **changing the world**.

HARRIET Tubman

Let's leave the last word on this to Harriet Tubman. Remember her? Our undersung shero? When she wasn't helping hundreds of slaves escape, she was saying wise and interesting things. One of those wise and interesting things was this:

"Always remember, you have within you the strength, the patience, and the passion to reach for the stars to change the world."

Sometimes those massive changes are so easily within our grasp. Think about the impact your smile has on someone who doesn't get smiled at very often.

Chapter 4

CODE RED

There's no point delaying it any longer.
We need to talk about periods.

Also known as the curse.

Or that time of the month.

Or having a visit from Aunt Flo.

Or surfing the crimson wave.

Or—perhaps the grossest code name of them all—

being   on   **the**   **rag.**

Nobody likes periods.

Nobody.

When I asked the girls in my focus group what was the SINGLE WORST THING about being a girl, they said this:

Periods!!!

<u>PEROIDS</u>*

period. (aaah!)

periods!

Period pain.

- -

* Peroids. EVERY BIT AS UNPLEASANT as periods.

Everyone agrees.

PERIODS
are a GIANT
NUISANCE!

But they are an essential feature of what makes you a **young woman** and not that little girl you used to be.

Periods may make you feel like **the living dead** for a couple of days each month—but once you start having them, your body is sending you a great big screaming red indicator that you now have **the miraculous ability to create life.**

In other words—if a little spermy visitor enters your body,

you
might
get
pregnant.

Got that?

Good.

Not that you need to worry about this until you're having sex. And, legally, **that shouldn't be any time before your sixteenth or eighteenth birthday** (depending on which state you live in). And even then, there is **no hurry**. But we'll discuss the sexy stuff in a separate chapter. Having your period and having sex are two topics that don't necessarily mix well.

Most girls have their first period between the ages of eleven and fourteen—but some girls may be as young as seven and others may be waiting until they're seventeen. If you're one of those late starters, you'll probably be **desperate** to join this mysterious **period club** that all your friends belong to. And then, one day, you'll look down into the toilet and wonder what the heck died. And you'll also wonder why you were **ever** in a hurry for this to happen.

So, what exactly are periods?

This is where it all gets a bit scientific . . .

A period is just one part of your **menstrual cycle**. This has nothing to do with bikes. It's about your reproductive system. Your reproductive system looks like this:

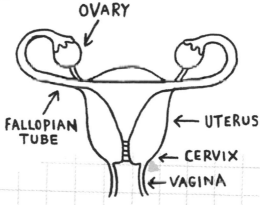

Day one of your menstrual cycle is the day that your period starts. Basically, your womb—or uterus—is having a cleaning day. This means throwing out a load of useless bloody junk. If you're lucky, this monthly clear-out will only last a couple of days. If your womb is **really** fanatical about cleaning, it could last a week. Perhaps even a bit longer. **Remember, we're all different.**

Eventually, the flow of useless bloody junk will stop. And that will be all you see of your menstrual cycle until day one comes around again about twenty-eight days later. Maybe a bit less than that. Maybe a bit more. **All different, remember?**

But even though the messy part is over, things are still happening inside you. After the period stops, your body starts releasing hormones. These hormones are telling your ovaries to release an egg.

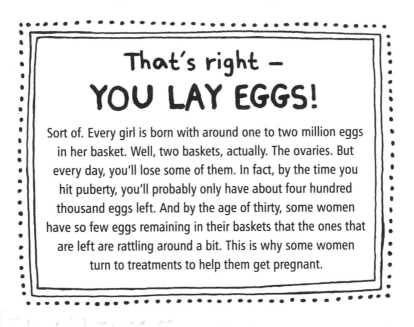

That's right –
YOU LAY EGGS!

Sort of. Every girl is born with around one to two million eggs in her basket. Well, two baskets, actually. The ovaries. But every day, you'll lose some of them. In fact, by the time you hit puberty, you'll probably only have about four hundred thousand eggs left. And by the age of thirty, some women have so few eggs remaining in their baskets that the ones that are left are rattling around a bit. This is why some women turn to treatments to help them get pregnant.

Your hormones are also telling your womb to get ready for an egg. If that egg is a **fertilized egg**, it's going to be staying for a while. Being the perfect hostess, the womb adds a bit of extra padding to its walls so that any fertilized egg will be all safe and snug in its comfy-cozy nest.

Meanwhile, one of your eggs starts to travel down your fallopian tube toward your womb. And then . . . almost always . . . **nothing happens.** Because unless your egg has hooked up with a spermy visitor, it won't be needed. And neither will all that extra comfy-cozy padding. So your womb has a cleaning day, throws the extra padding away, and the menstrual cycle starts all over again.

From an engineering perspective, your reproductive system is totally amazing.

From a **shoving-tampons-up-your-vagina** perspective, it's harder to actually care about this.

And that brings us nicely to . . .

Feminine hygiene products

Feminine hygiene products is the top secret code name* that
supermarkets and drugstores use to describe their crimson wave
collection. This is where you'll find everything you need to get you
through your monthly period. Let's go through this exciting range of
products one item at a time.

Pads

These are sold in packs. You
may already be intimate with
them. If you aren't, you soon
will be. Any day now, your
mom is going to knock on the
door of your bedroom, mutter
something incoherent, fling
a pack of pads on your bed,
and flee.

Or perhaps your mom is the
Big Day kind of mom? In
which case, she'll take you out to lunch, tell you it's a **Big Day**, and then
whisk you off to Walgreens so that you can buy your first pads together.

Either way, the pad is your starting point.

Pads come in all thicknesses. Beware of the words **panty liner, ultra thin,**
or **super slim**. These will be barely any thicker than a tissue—maybe ok for
the very start or end of your period—but no good at all for a **heavy flow**.

---

* You'll never see a sign saying Period Products. You just won't. It's like "period" is a dirty word or
  something. It's not. PERIOD.

Anything described as **regular** should do the job. If you find you need more, look for the words **super, super plus,** or **ultra.**

Some pads have **wings.** This is less exciting than you'd think. Wings are actually just flaps that wrap around your panties to hold the pad firmly in place. This may make you feel more secure if you want to do any vigorous activity.

Advantages:

☺ Pads are easy to use. You just pop them in your panties and away you go.

Disadvantages:

☹ They can be bulky. You'll have to figure out how to take them to the bathroom at school in maybe a sweater pocket or something.

☹ They have a sticky underside to keep them in place. If that sticky underside comes into contact with any of your pubic hairs, you'll know about it.

☹ It can feel like you've got a surfboard between your legs.

 Change your pad frequently.
You'll feel better, I assure you.

Tampons

These are sold in small boxes. This is what you'll turn to if you've fallen out of love with the pad. Perhaps you're already intimate with them. If so, you'll know that **intimate** is the key word here. Because a tampon sits right inside your vagina and absorbs all the goo and gunk that your womb throws out during its cleaning sessions. Basically, a tampon is a cross between a sponge and a plug.

So, really, it should be called a

splug or a
plonge.

But it isn't.

In Britain, some people call it a **mouse** because it's white and fluffy and has a tail. Actually, it's not a tail—it's a **cord**. And that cord is **massively important** because it's what you use to pull your tampon **out**.

Like pads, tampons come in different sizes and absorbencies: **light**, **regular**, and **super**. You can also find tampons called **super plus** or **ultra**. It's all fairly self-explanatory. But there are a few important rules:

1. Start small. Begin with a light. If this feels like it's going to fall right out, replace it with a regular. If the same happens, go super. It's important to get the right size to **match your flow**—and this will vary

from start to finish of your period. You **don't** want to be waddling around with a big old cotton torpedo inside you unnecessarily.

2. Make sure you know where that cord is. Pull it loose and get hold of it before you insert the tampon. You don't want to be left struggling to get the thing out again.*

3. As with pads, but even more importantly, **change tampons frequently**. Again, this is very, very important. Not only your comfort and hygiene but your health depends on this. Tampons are perfectly safe—but only if they are changed frequently. Every 3–4 hours is a good guide; you will soon learn what is right for you.

Tampons are inserted in one of two ways. Some come with an **applicator**—this is a handy little contraption made of two cardboard or plastic tubes. You push (gently!) the end of the big tube into your vagina and then push the smaller tube up into the larger one. This will magically put the tampon into just the exact position that it needs to be.

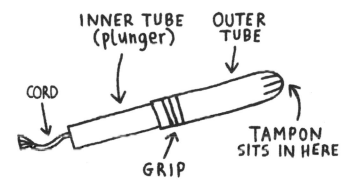

INNER TUBE (plunger) — OUTER TUBE — CORD — GRIP — TAMPON SITS IN HERE

---

* If this happens, the chances are that your tampon will just get over-full and gravity will cause it to fall out anyway. But if you really did get one stuck, you'd need to ask a trusted female adult to take you to a doctor. And just because she's one of us, insist on seeing a female doctor. She'll get it out for you. You can't have that thing hanging around inside you.

There are also tampons without applicators (look for the words "**non-applicator**"). These tampons are straightforward little things. You just push them into position with your fingertip (unwrap the plastic first, of course!).

Applicator vs Non-Applicator? YOU decide!

	Applicator	Non-Applicator
Advantages	☺ No blood on your fingers. ☺ Usually goes in the right direction.	☺ Fits in your purse. ☺ No nice tree was chopped down and turned into a tragic tampon applicator.
Disadvantages	☹ Bulkier, harder to fit in small purses. ☹ Takes a bit of practice. ☹ Leaves you with a lot of litter to dispose of. And you need to do this using the special bin that is (hopefully) provided in the stall. **You must not throw that applicator down the toilet.** Or else you'll block up the plumbing.	☹ Blood in your fingernails. ☹ Sometimes harder to go in. ☹ Needs at least as much practice as the applicator tampon.

The first time you try a tampon, you might find it a bit tricky. This is normal. Take your time and sit on the toilet or the edge of the bath if it helps. Relax and wiggle it around a little. It'll find its way into place eventually. And you'll know if it hasn't gone in correctly because you'll feel it and be waddling around like a penguin. So it's simple, really. All you have to do is remember that golden rule:

KEEP THE CORD OUT WHEN IT GOES IN!

And **HEY PRESTO!** You are properly tamponed-up.

Whether you use tampons or pads, always wash your hands before and after you attend to your private business.

Also, to make you feel more confident if you're worried that other people might **know** you're on your period,

take a bath or a shower every day during your period.

* * * * * * *

So, periods. They're a nuisance. But they're not **too** much of a pain, are they?

Um . . . yes. Sometimes.

The menstrual cycle is amazing and clever. Don't ever forget this. But, annoyingly, there are a couple of little glitches in the system.

At the time of their periods, some girls and women will experience **unpleasant design faults.** Some girls and women won't. **Because we're all different.**

The first glitch may happen just before the period starts. It'll be less of an obvious glitch and more of a feeling.

The sort of **feeling** that makes you **tired** or

annoyed

or

weepy

or

discombobulated*

or

REALLY STINKING FURIOUS.

- -

* Best word ever. It means confused and all out-of-sorts.

For no good reason that you can put your finger on.

And it gets better. Because alongside this delightful winning mood, you may find you have sore boobs and a splitting headache.

And then, Aunt Flo will come a-visiting.

Nice.

This helpful warm-up to the main act is known as PMS. Which stands for . . .

Premenstrual Syndrome

Many females will experience **some** of the symptoms of PMS but only a few will feel so bad that they want to scream at their own shadows. Mostly, these will be women in their late twenties to early forties.

The good news is that it never tends to last very long. Because when the crimson wave arrives, all PMS symptoms are usually swept away.

Oh. But then there's glitch number two.

Period pain

BOO!

Remember I said that your womb packs in extra padding each month in case it has to play host to a fertilized egg? And then, remember how I said it has a clear-out when the egg fails to show up? Well, to help push out all that unwanted lining, the womb makes itself smaller—which can feel to you like cramps. These **cramps** are sometimes so strong that you feel very uncomfortable. This uncomfortable unpleasantness is **period pain.**

Period pain often starts **before** you start bleeding. If you suffer from it, it will feel like an ache in your lower tummy. It may be dull and constant or it may be hour-long bursts of awfulness. Either way, you won't want to skip down the street singing, "I'm just gonna shake, shake, shake it off."

Actually, sufferers are more likely to be found floating between the bathroom and the sofa. Because—as well as that tummy ache—there are sometimes disruptions in your digestive system too.

Many females suffer from period pain at some point in their lives. Some girls and women go through this **awfulness** every single stinking month. It's a common problem. Unless the pain is seriously debilitating (and do tell your mom or doctor or other trusted adult if it is), it's just a message from Mother Nature that **there is no problem at all** and everything inside you is working just as it should.

Thanks for that, Mother Nature.

PMS and period pain may leave you alone. Or they may make you feel like the pits. But they shouldn't ever last very long or mess up your life so much that you can't go to school / drama class / karate practice / tapestry-weaving lessons.

So again, if cramps <u>are</u> messing up your life, tell your mom or that nice aunt or sympathetic older sister.

They won't be embarrassed because they've probably experienced a bit of PMS and period pain themselves. They can help you decide whether what you're feeling is the ordinary awfulness of periods or something that needs to be checked out by a doctor.

Don't sit by yourself and suffer in silence.

There's no need. Any woman with a heartbeat will have a fairly good idea how you feel.

Don't despair. There are things you can do to send period pain packing.

Turn the page for . . .

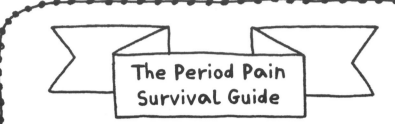

The Period Pain Survival Guide

Exercise. I know this sounds completely ridiculous, but actually, physical exercise can be a good way to keep period pain at bay. **Honestly!** As soon as your period starts, get on your bike or do some dance moves or take your dog for a walk. With a bit of luck, this may be all that's needed to stop period pain from sabotaging your life. At the least, the exercise endorphins will lift your spirits. It's worth a try!

Heat is often the most effective way to deal with period pain. Grab yourself a hot water bottle and curl up on the sofa. Heating pads (microwavable) or rice bran bags are also good for this. But make sure you don't overheat anything. You don't want to swap your cramps for a burn.

Bath. It's the same principle as above. Except that you're **inside** the heat. This will also get your parts nice and clean (see page 77), so you'll be getting two things done—all while you're also relaxing.

And if all else fails . . .

Painkillers from the drugstore. Again, ask your mom or doctor or another trusted adult. She'll know.

So is this chapter all doom and gloom?

Well . . . pretty much, yes . . . well, no, not totally . . . well . . . let's just say that there are a few crumbs of comfort. If you suffer from raging PMS and rampant period pain, that's **all** this comfort is. Tiny crumbs. But it's still something, isn't it?

I'll put them in great big font to make them less crumb-like.

1. You are a young woman.

Oh, yes, you are. So perhaps you're not yet old enough to vote, drink, drive a car, rent a Jet Ski, have sex, or get married, but—as far as nature is concerned—you are **all woman**!

2. Your period is a free bathroom pass.

Any day of the year. All you have to do is look panicked and whisper the words, "I really need to go to the bathroom." If your teacher is a human being, he or she will let you go. No questions asked.

3. Your period can get you out of PE.

Perfect for that day you're supposed to enjoy a cross-country run in a blizzard. You may need a note from a parent. And you may need to use this get-out-of-PE-card wisely and sparingly. Because **PE teachers have a weird habit of remembering the menstrual cycle of every single girl in the school**. The last thing you want is a referral to the school nurse for a chat about your **constant monster period**.

4. Your period is a totally valid reason for lounging around in sweatpants and hogging the sofa while eating cookies and watching bad TV.

Moms and sisters will understand. And dads and brothers will disappear faster than you can grumble the word "period."

From tiny crumbs, comforting cupcakes are made.

(OK, so it's still terrible. But if it helps, I'll share a piece of personal information with you. The entire time I was writing this chapter, I was **totally** on my period. I still got it done though, didn't I?!)

Chapter 5

FACE, FASHION, AND FIRST IMPRESSIONS

Beauty is only skin deep

Yes. OK. Agreed. But that thin layer of skin just happens to be what everybody notices about you **first**. So looking halfway decent is actually pretty important. In fact, according to recent research by some very brainy psychologists, it only takes **half a second** to create a first impression.*

It takes a while longer than that to change someone's bad opinion of you.

This may be unfair, shallow, and stupid—but it's also **the truth**.

First impressions are based on appearances. And **all** of us make these snap judgments. Even you, probably. Think about it. When you're in a dentist's waiting room or on a crowded bus or on a train and the only empty seats are next to random strangers—what do you do?

Do you:

1. Sit on the nearest empty seat. **No matter who's sitting next to you.**

2. Stand. Because there ain't **no way** you're sitting down next to any of those freaks.

3. Introduce yourself. Have a little chat. Get to know the real people behind the masks and **then** make your seat selection. Or . . .

4. Make a quick visual assessment of the seat situation and sit yourself down next to the person who looks a) the cleanest and b) the least like an ax murderer.

I bet you went with number four. Or number two if you're really on edge. Either way, you're making a **snap decision** based solely on what you can

---

* OK, maybe that half-a-second stuff is open to debate, but if you've got an issue with it, take it up with the brainy guys—not me. This research was jointly carried out by the University of Glasgow in Scotland and Princeton University in the United States. The final smarty-pants report is called "How Do You Say 'Hello'? Personality Impressions from Brief Novel Voices." It was published in 2014 and was written by Phil McAleer, Alexander Todorov, and Pascal Belin. So now you know.

see. Don't beat yourself up about it. It's just another knee-jerk reaction we've inherited from our cave-dwelling ancestors. Times were hard back then; we all needed to make on-the-spot judgments like this a billion times a day. Making a quick decision was the difference between staying alive and being chewed in half by a saber-toothed tiger.

Incidentally, if you went with option number one—**good for you!** There's not a shallow, judgmental bone in your body. Let's just hope the scowling yeti in the seat next to you behaves himself. Or, of course, *her*self.

If you went for option three, you'll probably end up sitting on your own anyway. See those people hurrying away? That's called **making a quick getaway**.

Anyway—like it or not—first impressions are a part of life. You might as well do what you can to try to create a good one.

Whoever you are, there are simple steps you can take to save yourself from a lifetime of watching people run away whenever you walk into a room. Let's begin with the most obvious and **easily** the most important.

Be clean

You don't want anyone to smell you before they see you. You just don't.

Take a bath or **shower every day**. Otherwise, you run the risk of smelling like toxic waste.

And don't think that a quick sniff under your pits is enough to keep the situation covered. It isn't. Most of us are actually **unaware of our own smell**. This means we could have body odor (BO) and **not even know it**.

Except that **you** are more at risk here than I am.

Because you're probably a teenager and I'm not. And that means you'll have those wild teenage **hormones** and overactive **sweat glands**. If those sweat glands get clogged with bacteria, everyone around you is going to know about it.

Take no chances.

Washing with soap **every day** will remove your sweat **and** those reeking bacteria. Pay particular attention to your armpits, your front bottom, your back bottom, and your feet.

And while we're on the subject, it's a good idea to give your neck a good scrub with a washcloth. This will keep you from getting a nasty yellow sweat mark inside your collar. Then when you're done, dry yourself thoroughly and treat yourself to a couple of swipes of deodorant.

I'm sorry if all this has just made me sound like your mom. But at least it means we both care about you.

So that was easy. Now be sure not to undo all that good clean work by putting on sweaty, stinky clothes. Remember:

If your clothes smell like moldy cheese, so will YOU.

Good personal hygiene is essential. Everything else is mere decoration.

The truth about faces

Hardly anyone is satisfied with the one they've got. Not even the "beautiful" people on TV. That's why so many of them are always getting bits snipped off and altered. I don't advise you to do this. I advise you to learn to like the face you have. It may not be your idea of perfect—but it's unique and it's natural and it's interesting. And if you can turn your face into the type of face that **smiles a lot**, I promise you, **people will think you're attractive**. It's better to have a nose like a spud and a lush lovely smile than be a vision of perfection **and** be Bellatrix Lestrange. Or the Snow Queen. Or any other beautiful but vile witch.

Which brings us to **teeth**. It's obvious, but clean them, OK? Morning and night. That attractive smile will be totally **wrecked** if it has bits of bacon jammed in the cracks.

But what if I have ugly, hideous braces?

Smile wider. You're getting your crooked teeth fixed while you're still young and your parents are paying for it. Smart move, sister! When those braces come off, your smile is going to be **absolutely stunning**. So you'd better get some smiling practice in fast.

A friendly, smiling face is a **win**. But—hey—we're girls, and if we want to add a few finishing flourishes to ourselves with a makeup brush, we can. And this is one aspect of life where being a girl really **does** give you some sort of an advantage.

Makeup

Girls are pretty much free to decorate themselves as they like. If we want shiny, luscious lips, we can dab on a bit of lip gloss. If we want to look less dead, we can put on a touch of blush. If we want eyelashes that aren't beige, we just whip out the mascara. Done.

If a boy even **speaks** of such things, there's a high likelihood that someone will instantly accuse him of being gay.

It's not fair.

Then again, some girls feel **under pressure** to paint their lips and brighten up their cheekbones and give themselves wickedly long eyelashes. From TV and from films and from magazines and from boys and from their parents and from the internet and from random passersby in the street and—most of all—from other girls in their classes. And that's not fair either.

When I asked the female folk in my Student Focus Group to write down the **best** things about being a girl, some of them wrote things like this:

Getting to use make up and hair accessories.

And when I asked them to write down the **worst** things, some others wrote things like this:

• Having to do hair + make-up everyday!

Well, guess what? You don't **have** to do anything. Be a lioness, remember. Have the courage to be the person you **want** to be.

My suggestion is that you look at it this way:

Makeup exists. Some of us like wearing it and some of us don't. And it's fine either way because **we're all different**. But at least we get to make that choice.

But be careful. Applying makeup is an art. That's why there are trained professional people called **makeup artists**. If—like me—you have no natural skills in this area, it's best to follow this age-old piece of wisdom:

LESS IS MORE.

You don't want to look like a birthday cake.

Here are a few more dos and don'ts to help you avoid any disasters.

MAKEUP DOS

1. **Use the shade of concealer or foundation that most closely matches your skin tone.** Try before you buy with those little tester tubes you find at the store. **You're better off wearing no concealer or foundation at all than wearing the wrong shade.** Take a pocket mirror with you into the store and apply a little of the tester to your jawline. (The back of your hand isn't actually helpful because the skin there probably isn't the same color as your face.) If you've got the right shade, the makeup should pretty much disappear into your skin so you can't really see you're wearing any makeup at all. If this happens, it's a **WIN**. Just make sure you:

2. **Rub it in**. Otherwise you'll look pixelated.

3. **Check out your handiwork before you leave your house.** If you can see a line of makeup, rub it in a bit more.

4. **Store your makeup in a clean, dry place.** And ...

5. **Keep your eyeliner and mascara especially clean.** You don't want to give yourself a gross, gunky eye infection.

6. **Clean off your makeup completely <u>every night</u> before you go to bed.** Otherwise it stops being makeup and becomes dirt. (Soap and water is fine for washing away everyday grime but is likely to hurt A LOT if it gets into your eyes. So use eye makeup remover for mascara.)

MAKEUP DON'TS

1. **Don't make yourself look orange.** Unless you want to look like an Oompa-Loompa.

2. **Don't get too carried away with the mascara.** You want your eyelashes to look long, not crunchy. If you can hear your eyelashes when you blink, you've overdone it.

3. **Don't plaster makeup on top of pimples.** Remember what we said about the vicious circle? If you have a pimple, you shouldn't put more than a little concealer on it—at the most.

4. **Don't plaster makeup.** You're a young person, not a run-down building. You don't need Spackle.

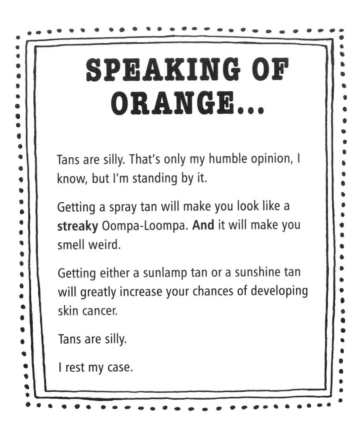

SPEAKING OF ORANGE...

Tans are silly. That's only my humble opinion, I know, but I'm standing by it.

Getting a spray tan will make you look like a **streaky** Oompa-Loompa. **And** it will make you smell weird.

Getting either a sunlamp tan or a sunshine tan will greatly increase your chances of developing skin cancer.

Tans are silly.

I rest my case.

I'll give the last word on makeup to the boys. Obviously you're not wearing it for **them**. You're wearing it for yourself. But it's always interesting to know what the other half of the population thinks. One of the boys in my Student Focus Group told me he prefers girls who . . .

Don't plummet teemselves in make up.

Yep. Plummeting is a poor strategy. So is plastering.

So you're clean. You don't smell. And you've got a smile on your face. Yippee. All these things will help you get on in the world. Now let's talk about . . .

~~~~~~~~~~~~~~~~~~~~~~~~~~~~

Fashion

It's a labyrinth.

And for girls especially, it can be incredibly stressful.

Picture the scene: the menswear department of your favorite store. All the shirts are nicely folded and arranged in neat piles on tables. A few T-shirts are hanging on a rail. A suited assistant is hovering nearby to help "sir" select a pair of jeans. Cool head-nodding music is playing . . .

And now picture the women's clothing section in the exact same store. T-shirts, sweatshirts, dresses, crop tops, party tops, leggings, sweatpants, yoga pants, hot pants, cargo pants, capri pants, and jeans are all jumbled together in a massive messy heap on a "display" stand. Some of them have smears of orange makeup on them. Thumping club music is playing so loudly you can't think. Clothing racks are so crammed that you can't get a good view of what you're looking at. But—hey—that sleeve looks **super nice**! And then, when you pull it free from the rack, you see that what you're holding is an utterly pointless cardigan-type-thing. Which is **sort of like** a cardigan   but only if you've got no body.*

---

* That would be a shrug. Apparently.

This is how females do shopping. And—just as it is with makeup—opinion is totally split down the middle. Some of us think it's exciting and fabulous—after all, compared to the boys, our clothing options are endless. But some of us just want an ordinary cardigan that covers our bodies as well as our arms.

What we wear says **a lot** about who we are. And it really doesn't matter whether it's a pricey designer label or something we found in a thrift store—so long as it **works** for us. Because clothes are packaging. They have a job to do. Ideally they should:

 Stop us from freezing or melting or suffering any other sort of environmental damage.

 Make us look appealing. And if that sounds shallow, think of it this way. Do you really want to wear things that make you seem repulsive to other people?

If both those boxes are checked, your outfit is a **winner**.

I can't tell you what to wear. I have enough problems dressing myself. And besides—**everyone's different**. But if you're **happy** with what you're wearing and the people around you are **happy** to be seen with you, then you're wearing it well. Here are a few more of those one-size **dos** and **don'ts** that fit everybody.

WARDROBE DOS

1. **Buy stuff that fits.** In **your** size. Not the size you'd like to be. <u>This is so important</u>. Clothes only look good when they fit properly. Wear something too small and it will squeeze you in all the wrong places and make you look like you're made of marshmallows. And then it'll probably rip. But wear something too big and you run the risk of looking like a pregnant lady. **Just wear the right size**. No one but **you** is going to see the size tag anyway.

2. **Be a master of fashion.** Not a slave to it. It's a **fact** that some fashion trends are totally unflattering and make people look **ridonkulous**. Don't believe me? Dig out some old pictures of your parents and see what they were wearing when they were your age. Or better still, dig out some photos of yourself from just a few years back. Feel like wearing that outfit now? Nope. Didn't think so. So if you suspect you look like an overgrown toddler in that leopard-print romper, trust your eyes and choose another outfit. A master of fashion wears **what suits her best**. Not whatever the latest craze is.

3. **Be creative.** Fashion is art. You don't need to spend billions of dollars to look cool. A few original touches can make your favorite $10 party dress look totally yours.

WARDROBE DON'TS

1. **Don't wear every color all at once.** True, it's good not to be beige. You don't want your clothes to act as camouflage. But then again, you don't want people to mistake you for someone called Rainbow Rhonda, who juggles at kids' parties.*

2. **Don't blatantly copy other people.** It'll annoy them. And even if they can't be annoyed because they don't know you're doing it, it's still a bad policy. There's no point wearing what Selena Gomez wore in the latest *Teen Vogue* to school the following Monday. You'll look like a copy cat. You'll always look better if you are **being yourself**.

3. **Don't wear a black bra under a white top.** Not good.

4. **Don't wear no bra under a see-through / tight top**. Why would you?

5. **Don't have pockets longer than your outfit**. If your pockets hang down longer than the legs of your shorts, I'd suggest that maybe your shorts are a tad too short.

* Unless you do. And to be fair, some people pull off this look with real style and charisma. Just be prepared for people to think you are "crazy."

Perhaps those **don'ts** have made me sound like a crusty old fossil. Perhaps you think we should all just forget about rules and wear whatever the heck we want. Well, maybe. But whatever we choose to do, it's always a good idea to be aware of something called . . .

Semiotics

This is a flashy word meaning the **study and interpretation of signs.** Some very brainy individuals think that **everything** is a sign and **everything** can be read. Just like a book. And maybe there's some truth in that, because if I saw a grown man strolling through town in nothing but his underwear, I'd read his outfit and think, *Yikes! What a weirdo!*

What would **you** think?

Intentionally or not, our clothes send out messages that other people read. It's a smart idea to know exactly what those messages are. And to make sure we're cool with them.

WALK LIKE A WINNER

This chapter wouldn't be complete without a quick comment on shoes. Lots of us girls **love** shoes. And compared to the boys, we've got a **huge** selection to choose from. We can wear ballet flats and oxfords and tennis shoes and moccasins and kitten heels and wedges and flip-flops and sandals and sling-backs and loafers and all sorts of footwear things. Though, if you're like me, you're more of a boot and sneaker type. Either way, what we wear on our feet is mightily important. Because if we get it wrong, we'll be waddling around like toddlers. And while that may be very cute for two-year-olds, it's not ideal for teenagers.

Here's the thing.

Wear whatever you want on your feet so long as you can comfortably walk in them.

This is especially true for high heels. Although, I confess that I'm no expert in this field. Despite being five feet tall and **not** growing, I've never worn a pair of high heels in my life. So I had a chat with my friend Donna, who wears the tallest shoes in the world. She said this:

> Wearing high heels is like stilt—walking. Go higher gradually. Begin with a low heel and increase your heel height just a little with each new pair of shoes. Otherwise, you could end up looking like Bambi on ice.

Wise advice. Donna also said this:

> The higher you get, the more your toes will be shoved forward into very narrow spaces. This is likely to leave you with cuts and blisters and possible foot deformity.

So there you go.

A few extra inches vs. possible foot deformity.

Choose carefully.

The great weight debate

Magazines and newspapers are always sending out messages about the human body. (Remember the pressure messages we talked about in Chapter 1?) Every time we see women's clothes being modeled, it's always by some super-skinny, super-tall model who looks nothing like 99.9 percent of the other women on our planet. This is annoying. It's also stupid and potentially dangerous because it promotes the idea that—in order to look good—girls and women should always be exceptionally thin.

To look good, we need to be a **healthy weight** for our age and height. A good guideline for this is the **Body Mass Index.*** If we're below or above a healthy BMI range, we may be putting ourselves at risk from possible health issues.

It's not rocket science.

A balanced diet + exercise = a healthy body.

And **some** of those models you see in magazines **aren't** healthy. They've artificially achieved that level of skinniness by eating pretty much nothing.

And that's not right.

As you get older, you often develop a few curves. Be proud of them.

---

* If you're not sure what this is, have a look at the NIH website: www.nhlbi.nih.gov. There's a really good BMI calculator that can help you check that you're within a healthy range.

Looking good online

So now you're clean. You don't smell. You've got a smile on your face. You're **not** dressed like Rainbow Rhonda and you can walk around without falling over. Hooray! **Nothing can go wrong.** Your glowing first impression is guaranteed.

Oh . . .
Except . . .

Except there's that **one** embarrassing picture of you online. The one where you're posing in a pair of zebra-print leggings and a push-up bra. Lady Gaga style.

And **every one** of your nine hundred and thirty-four online "friends" is free to view it whenever they like. And if any of them SHARE it or LIKE it or LEAVE A COMMENT, then all their friends can enjoy your Gaga moment too.

DON'T LET SELFIES RUIN YOUR IMAGE.

It's important to hold it together in the real world—but we need to hold it together in the digital world too. I've got news for you:

Social networking sites aren't as private as you might think.

And every picture you upload and every status update you write becomes part of your **digital footprint** and exists—somewhere—in cyberspace **forever**. Even if you've deleted it and shut down your account.

The only **real way** to be safe online is simple. **Don't post any personal details about your life**—like your address or your phone number or your date of birth. And **don't post any images that you're not comfortable with every inhabitant of planet Earth seeing**. Facebook and Instagram are jam-packed with selfies. And while many of these are random pictures of people's fingernails, quite a lot are also body shots involving girls wearing barely any clothes. This is where it all gets so serious that I need another black box . . .

> Don't even **THINK** about posting a nude picture of yourself online. Or sending one to some hot boy's phone. **If, legally*, you are still a child, then your naked selfie is actually an INDECENT PICTURE OF A CHILD**. And that's *illegal*. Even if that "child" in the picture is YOU! And any hot boy who receives it would be breaking the law too—for having an indecent image of a child (YOU) on his phone. Oh, and guess what? If you're under sixteen, the Gaga-in-her-undies snap is likely to be illegal as well. Because—you guessed it—it's an indecent picture of a child.

Even if these selfies seem funny and cool now, **they won't be so funny and cool in five or ten or twenty-five years' time when you're applying to colleges, or to your first job, or running for president of the United States.**

This chapter has turned out to be quite complicated, hasn't it? I'm going to leave you with two far simpler thoughts before I move on.

* The age when you are recognized as an adult will vary from sixteen to eighteen years old depending on which state you live in.

Thought #1

Fashion is temporary.

Yes it is. By very definition. As soon as something is popular, it's pretty much on its way out again. So think very carefully before you make any permanent changes to your personal appearance. Tattoos are not temporary. Anyone who wants to get rid of one has to undergo repeated, expensive, and painful cosmetic surgery or laser treatment. And that goes for ear stretching too—or ear gouging to give it its more delightful name. It might seem like a good idea now. But so did mullets once.

Thought #2

Looking great is a mental state.

Yes it is. It's a frame of mind. If you're feeling hunky-dory inside, it's more than likely that you'll look hunky-dory on the outside too. By the way, the singer, songwriter, rapper, and eternally cool hipster Neneh Cherry expresses this very point in her hit song "Buffalo Stance." Go and check her out right now. There roars a lioness if ever I heard one.

Chapter 6
THE HAIR NECESSITIES

Hair is a big deal for us girls. In fact, it's our crowning glory. And we know it. That's why we're always brushing it, washing it, styling it, straightening it, dyeing it, and doing it. At times, it even halts the smooth-running flow of our everyday lives. Ever had a conversation like this?

> If you want a ride, you'd better hurry up. I don't have all day.

> I can't hurry up. I'm doing my hair.

> You'll have to walk then!

> Yeah. Whatevs.

> Ugh. That is TOTALLY another tardy slip coming my way.

You don't hear boys talking about **doing** their hair, do you? You just don't. At the most, you might hear them mutter something about "smoothing it down."

Doing your hair is a typically female thing. And it can take up a heckuva lot of time, trouble, and cash. For some girls, this sacrifice is no sacrifice at all. Because **doing** their hair is a sweet joy and a pleasure. But for many other girls, it's the bore of all bores. It's not even easy to "opt out" of **doing** one's hair. Because even if we think . . .

. . . chances are that we'll **still** feel some sort of hair anxiety. Because somebody somewhere will make us feel that we absolutely **should** be **doing** it.

Yep. I'm afraid **we're even under pressure from our own hair**.

But there **is** a flip side to all of this. Unlike a lot of smooth-headed males, we get to keep ours pretty much forever . . .

. . . provided it **is** on our head, of course. If a hair dares to sprout up anywhere else, it's **a whole other issue.**

You know those **pressure messages** we talked about earlier? Way back in Chapter 1?

Well, they will already be sending you a crystal-clear instruction:

Any hair that's NOT on your head must GO!

This means that most of us will spend an entire lifetime obsessively shaving it off. And I speak from experience when I tell you that **that's** a pain too.

But that's not helpful. Sorry.

Try not to think of it as a pain. Try to think of it as **your** independent decision regarding your body hair. Because if you really **don't want** to shave or wax or pluck or trim or smother yourself in hair removal cream, then **DON'T**. But we'll come to that later. First up, let's address any concerns you may have about . . .

The hair on your head

Maybe you don't have any concerns. Maybe your hair is soft and shining and beautiful and gorgeous. Maybe it's even **lustrous**?

Lucky you!

You may as well skip this section.

But if hair worries sometimes make your head spin, **stay right here**. I've got news for you.

HARDLY ANYONE LIKES HER OWN HAIR.

And that includes the "beautiful" people on TV. That's why so many of them are always having it extended or cropped or dyed or bleached or curled or straightened. You are **not alone** with your feelings of hair rage. In fact, most of us travel through life eyeing other people's locks with envy. I do it. I wish I had my friend Tara's hair. I've wished that for about twenty years. Hers is sleek and straight and shiny and dark. Mine is like a beige head beard. It's high time me and Tara did a swap.

But the weirdest thing is this:

Sometimes people have complimented me on my "lovely thick head of hair."

That may be a little strange. That may be a little *wrong*—but it also means that it's **an absolute certainty** that

SOMEBODY somewhere LOVES YOUR hair.

So please try not to be so hard on yourself.

It helps, too, if you **get to know your own hair type** and work with it—rather than wrestle it into submission. There's no point. Your hair will always grow back fighting. The type of hair we have depends on our parents. If either of them has sleek, straight, shiny, dark hair, there's a reasonable chance that we will have it too. Then again, if one of them has a beige head beard, we might get stuck with that. Or perhaps we'll have some sort of weird fusion of the two.

In loving hands, ANY type of hair can look lovely.

Now, I am **no expert** in this field of knowledge. **This is not a beauty manual and I am not a beauty expert.**

But because I care and because I wanted to save you a lot of time, I typed the words HAIR CARE into Google.

There were

four-hundred-and-ninety-seven million

results. I read them all.

And then I condensed the whole 497,000,000 pages into the following "Hair Map."*

Excuse me, but it needs a whole page.

---

* Hair Map© is the copyright of Hayley Long. You saw it here first. Hair Map.

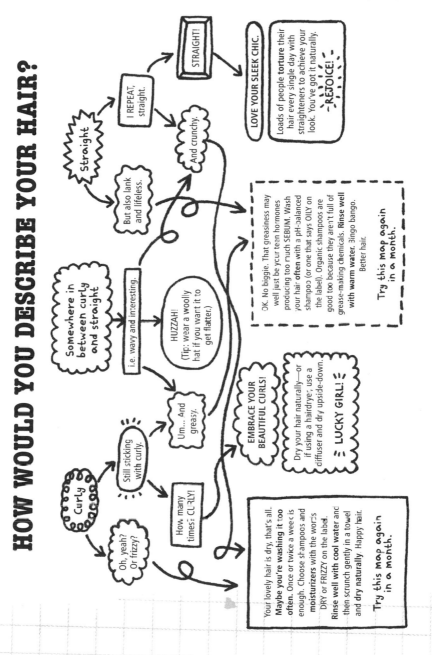

HOW WOULD YOU DESCRIBE YOUR HAIR?

Straight

But also lank and lifeless.

I REPEAT, straight.

And crunchy.

STRAIGHT!

LOVE YOUR SLEEK CHIC.

Loads of people torture their hair every single day with straighteners to achieve your look. You've got it naturally. ~REJOICE!~

Somewhere in between curly and straight

i.e. wavy and interesting.

HUZZAH! (Tip: wear a woolly hat if you want it to get flatter.)

Um... And greasy.

OK. No biggie. That greasiness may well just be your teen hormones producing too much SEBUM. Wash your hair **often** with a pH-balanced shampoo (or one that says OILY on the label). Organic shampoos are good too because they aren't full of grease-making chemicals. **Rinse well with warm water.** Bingo bango. Better hair.

Try this map again in a month.

Curly

Oh, yeah? Or frizzy?

Still sticking with curly.

How many times: CURLY!

EMBRACE YOUR BEAUTIFUL CURLS!

Dry your hair naturally—or if using a hairdryer, use a diffuser and dry upside-down.

~LUCKY GIRL!~

Your lovely hair is dry, that's all. **Maybe you're washing it too often.** Once or twice a week is enough. Choose shampoos and **moisturizers** with the words DRY or FRIZZY on the label. **Rinse well with cool water** and then scrunch gently in a towel and dry naturally. Happy hair.

Try this map again in a month.

See. All hair is **good** hair. Be happy with what you've got.

> But
> the longer the
> hair, the more
> gorgeous the girl,
> surely?

Oh, hush.

Well-tended long hair *is* lovely and looks very feminine. But exactly the same can be said of short hair too.

Life isn't a fairy tale and we don't live in stone towers waiting for handsome princes to rescue us by climbing up our braided hair. **Have your hair cut or styled in whatever way makes you happy**. After all, it's **you** who has to live with it. Not anyone else. And anyway, not everyone has the type of hair that **will** grow long.

Some hair just wants to grow outward, like Albert Einstein's.

If your hair does this, the words **"pixie cut"** are a precious gift.

Whatever style you opt for, a **regular trim** is a good idea. This will rid you of split ends and keep your hair looking attractive and healthy.

A WORD OF CLIPPING CAUTION THOUGH . . .

Beware of any "trending" hairdo of the moment. It will be out of date faster than yesterday's Twitter update. OK, so your hair grows out quickly. But your mom will keep that incriminating school photo **forever**.

Having said that, <u>no haircut poses any serious risk of long-lasting psychological trauma</u>. Not when you look at it like this:

The difference between a tragic disaster cut and a happy haircut is only ABOUT THREE WEEKS.

At the most.

Because, by then, your hair will have grown a bit and you'll have gotten used to it.

End of trauma.

So, there. Our hair is lovely. And we're all going to love it just the way it is and let it do its natural thing.

Dream on...

Like that's actually going to happen!

Let's **get real** and move on to the bit about . . .

Straighteners

These are **not good** for your hair. Maybe they're even **bad** for it. I've arrived at this conclusion after reading 497,000,000 HAIR CARE results on Google.

Also, my hairdresser always makes a really disgusted face whenever the S-word is mentioned. **Also**, I happen to know that straighteners are **highly addictive**. And the reason I know this is because I, personally, cannot cope without one. It's true. No matter how many times I stare at my own Hair Map© and read the words **wavy** and **interesting**, I still look in the mirror and see a big beige head beard.

Straighteners help remove this image.

So if YOU TOO have an unhealthy dependency on hot metal, the following information box may be of use.

HOW TO USE A STRAIGHTENER WITHOUT BURNING A HOLE IN YOUR HEAD—OR ANYTHING ELSE

1. Before you buy any straightener, look to see if the word CERAMIC is printed on the packaging. This is important. If it is, it means your straightener will be a bit more expensive—but on the upside, it means you're less likely to end up with frazzled, smoking hair.

2. Don't think of it as a hair straightener. Think of it as a **Weapon of Mass Destruction**. This will help you to handle it with care and will also encourage you to steer clear of your ears.

3. ALWAYS use a heat protection spray or serum on your hair BEFORE you start ironing.

4. Pull your hair upward as you straighten and DO IT AS QUICKLY AS YOU CAN. This will a) give your hair a bit of volume and keep it from looking like two sheets of uncooked lasagna, and b) keep it from acquiring the texture of a pork rind.

5. If you ever **do** see smoke or smell burned hair, **switch that thing off immediately**.

6. In any case, **turn your straightener off** when you've finished using it.

7. Unplug it from the wall too. Just to be extra safe.

8. Don't leave a straightener on your carpet / floor / dresser / bed / cat. Straighteners can reach temperatures of 428°F. That's more than hot enough to inflict a nasty scorch mark. Or start a fire!

But the best advice of all is this:

BE KIND.
GIVE YOUR HAIR A
HEAT HOLIDAY
SOMETIMES.

By the way, pretty much everything you've just read applies if you're using a **curling iron** too.

And now for a rare glimpse inside my mind . . .

Give your hair a heat holiday? Did I just write that?

Ohmygosh— I am such a hypocrite!

Yeah, but at least I've tamed my head beard.

It's still totally beige though, Hayley.

HAIR SPRAY, HAIR WAX, HAIR MUD, AND HAIR GEL

Go easy on this stuff. Do you really want to look like you've got Lego hair? A couple of squirts of spray or a tiny blob of wax, mud, or gel rubbed onto your fingertips is **enough**. Use too much and you'll smell like cheap bubble gum. And besides, how is anyone gorgeous ever going to run their fingers through your hair if you've glued all of it together?

The hair in other places

It's weird.

In popular Western culture—that's North America, Europe, Australia, and New Zealand—females get bombarded with Pressure Messages telling them that they really should have long hair. Like Rapunzel. Or Barbie. Or Beyoncé. Or almost any royal person who doesn't happen to be a guy.

Western culture **loves** long-haired women.

It's less happy about **hairy women**.

Make no mistake about it, long-haired and hairy are **not** the same thing.

Oh my gosh, NO!

Hairy is an **entirely different** state of affairs. In fact, it actually seems like there's little a woman can do to cause greater **offense** and

⊚ **SHOCK** ⊚

and **moral outrage**

. . . than allowing a hairy patch to sprout out from under her armpit.

(Honestly, the fallout from that viral photo of you wearing those zebra-print Lady Gaga leggings would be less traumatic to deal with.)

And this must mean that nature has seriously **messed up** somewhere. Because as soon as those teenage hormones kick in, girls start sprouting hair in **all sorts** of places.

So that means we're all tragic hairy freaks then?

Of course not!

What it **means** is that—in spite of what society says—being a bit hairy is normal.

I'll say it again. **Body hair is normal.**

Got that?

Good. So try to stop seeing your body hair as something disgusting. It's not. It's just **there**—on your body. The same as eyelashes are on your eyelids and nails are on your fingers and toes.

Here's another thing:

There are NO proven biological benefits or hygienic reasons to remove your body hair.

So if you want to get rid of it—fine. But if you don't—**that's fine too**.

Honestly.

Whoa, there! Stop!

I thought bushy body hair was strictly the domain of man-hating feminists and Lesbians???

First of all, let's not assume that feminists and lesbians hate men. They don't. And let's **also** not assume that **every** feminist and **every** lesbian shares the exact same views on body hair. Angelina Jolie is often described as a feminist. She's also very open about the fact that she's had a lesbian relationship. Does she look especially hairy to you?

Secondly, our relationship with our body hair is complicated.

Get yourself ready for a quick brain workout . . .

A few theories regarding your body hair

From a feminist's perspective, it all boils down to something like this:

The only reason you think your body hair is butch and ugly is because you've been **encouraged** to think it. **I've** been encouraged to think it too. About mine, I mean. In fact, all of us older girls and women are programmed to be **scared of our own body hair**.

Professor Susan Basow is a very smart American psychologist. She reckons that the **man's world** we live in (remember what we talked about in Chapter 2?) is deliberately sending out a false and shady message to make women feel inferior to men. Professor Basow says:

". . . the implication of the hairlessness norm is that women's bodies are not attractive when natural, and must be modified."

In other words, the message is that women must remove their body hair because women's natural bodies aren't as good as men's natural bodies. (You never see guys worried about their hairy arms and legs, do you?)

In other words, males are better than females.

In other words, **it's a man's world**.

But that's just one point of view.

Which is fine. As is this **other** way of looking at it:

We choose to shave and pluck and trim and wax simply because we think it looks nice.

And that's absolutely **fair enough**.

So long as it **is** still a choice.

Because when it's **no longer** a choice—when we're actually just reacting to **really intense peer pressure** and the fear of being pointed at and labeled **Hairy Mary**—then that's no better than girl-on-girl bullying, isn't it?

Hmm?

Should it stay or should it go?

Once you start fussing around with your body hair, you'll be fussing with it forever.

So don't start that fussing until you're good and ready. And—seriously— why not have a chat about it with your mom first? She was just like you once. In a way, she's your hairy prototype. Why bother to reenact all her plucking disasters? If she advises you to wait a while, she's probably right.

But ultimately it's your call. If you **want** to pluck your eyebrows and shave your pits and legs—do it.

And if you don't, good for you—skip ahead to the next chapter. But you might want to **read the following information box first**.

A BRUTAL REALITY CHECK

I stand by everything I've just said. About choices. And about it being YOUR decision. No question. But I need you to understand that **some** decisions create challenges. Very little in this life is hassle-free. So which heap of hassle are you going to take on?

Fighting your body hair or fighting the tide of public opinion?

Choose your battles wisely. Your right to have hair under your arms may seem like a big, important issue or it may not. But let those tufts be seen in public and it may be a big deal to some **snarky people**. If this doesn't faze you and you want to fight for your right to be hairy, I salute you. Off you go now and wait for me at the next chapter. If, on the other hand, there is any possibility that your body hair is coming off, I'll meet you just on the other side of this gray box.

Now, let's take it from the top:

Eyebrows *

Basically, I think it's safe to assume that we all want two of them. The bald patch of skin that is usually found between them is called the **glabella.**

Did you know that? Nope—me neither until about ten seconds ago.

If your eyebrows are trying to meet up and have a party, you can sort it out yourself in three relatively simple moves.

---

* Take a look sometime at the models in fashion advertising and magazines—see their eyebrows? You'll probably notice that thick, luxuriant, quite bushy brows are all the rage. So much so that many women with naturally thinner brows try to enhance theirs with eyebrow pencils and powders. So if you're lucky enough to be prominently browed, think twice before messing with yours!

1. Run a **clean washcloth** under a warm tap.

2. Lay the warm washcloth across your eyebrows. The warmth and steam will open up your pores. This means that those pesky glabella-invading hairs will come out of your face with less pain.

3. Using a **clean, sharp pair of tweezers**, pull out any unwelcome glabella dwellers.

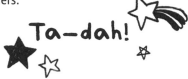

Ta-dah!

Two eyebrows.

HAZARD WARNING!

Your glabella really is just that bit above the bridge of your nose.
Don't be tempted to make it wider.
PUT THE TWEEZERS DOWN NOW.

That was the easy bit. But what do you want to do next?

Just a quick clean-up will do for me, Hayley. But with a couple of fierce lines shaved in—rapper style.

Shave them off completely and draw them on again with an eyebrow pencil.

WHOA THERE!

Whatever you have in mind—even if it's just a little bit of reshaping—don't rush into anything without knowing exactly what you are doing. Your eyebrows are **massively important**. Because they're on your face. Mess them up and you could look lopsided. Get out the marker or the brow pencil or the deluxe-fluid-finishing-definer and you could look like you've got two big black slugs sucking up to your brows. Pluck them too hard and you could spend the rest of your life looking shocked.

SHUDDER. Remember that note on page 128! Many of the biggest movie stars and pop stars proudly sport thick, luxuriant eyebrows. Lustrous, even. So if you are lucky enough to have thick eyebrows naturally, why mess with them? Even the hairs that stray into your glabella!

Upper lip

Despite what the world says, most females have a bit of hair here. Often, it's so pale and fine that nobody except you will ever notice it. If this is the case, why worry about it? For girls who have naturally dark hair though, these fuzzies may be a bit more noticeable.

No worries. **Ask your mom or helpful older sister to help you** and choose from one of the following options.

1. **Facial bleach.** The drugstore will sell bleach that is especially designed for facial hair. And guess where you'll find it? On the shelf with all the other facial and skincare products for women. **Because facial hair on women is normal and common.** The bleach is easy to use and won't take long. **But make sure you properly follow the instructions.**

Whatever else you do with your life, DO NOT put any other type of bleach on your face or body EVER. NOT EVER.

2. **Facial wax.** A facial hair waxing kit—that's what you need. And it's there on the same drugstore shelf right near the facial bleach. This will **only** work if those hairs on your upper lip are quite long. Hot or cold wax is involved. And a quick sharp tug. But it may make you shout . . .

Yes, it hurts as much as it sounds. Again, **read the instructions carefully.**

3. **Facial hair removal cream.** You've guessed it. It's on the same shelf as the bleach and the wax. Smells like a horrible accident in a chemistry lab. Easy peasy pain-freesy. **But follow the instructions carefully.**

Armpits and legs

Yes indeed. Come summer and the season of the tank top, it takes a lot of **inner strength** to let those pit-hairs grow. The same can be said of the hairy-legged shorts-wearer. So if you see a female with body hair, **please** don't be one of the frightened people who sighs an **"Ugggh"** and shakes her head. That hairy girl or woman is a **warrior**. She is taking on the world in order to be her natural self. Respect. And if you are one of those warriors yourself, double respect!

If you are not (and this is totally fine too), there are four options:

1. **Wax.** As before. Will hurt. Your underarm is a particularly sensitive area.

2. **Hair removal cream.** Will stink of rotting zombies.

3. **The epilator.** This is a small, electronic, handheld contraption, which costs anything from a few bucks—for a really cheap one—to a hundred dollars for a hi-tech, razzley-dazzley one. The epilator has metal springs on one end, which vibrate or rotate really quickly and **yank** your unwanted hairs right out of your body. Does this process hurt? **OhMyGoshYes!**

4. **The razor.** The most common, cheapest, and easiest. If you've never done this before, don't worry, it's simple. But as always, take care, and observe the six following steps.

SIX STEPS TO WET SHAVING

You will need:

A clean disposable razor. Women's razors are available but the only key difference between these and any others is the color—pink. Blue ones work just as well!

Hot water.

Soap or shaving cream.

The best place to do this is in the bath but you can stand by the sink too.

Method:

1. Lather the soap until it's nice and foamy. Generously cover your hairy area in foamy soap (or shaving cream).

2. If shaving your armpit, raise your arm above your head so the skin is nice and taut. If doing a leg, lift it out of the water.

3. Gently glide the razor along the surface of your skin **against the direction of the hair growth.**

4. Rinse razor thoroughly and repeat.

5. Dry skin carefully.

6. If you've shaved your legs, apply a skin moisturizer or body lotion to stop your legs from getting all flaky. If you've shaved your armpits, **don't apply anything to your underarm for at least a couple of hours.** Especially deodorant. Or it'll hurt A LOT.

Notice this said **wet** shaving? Don't ever scrape away at your body with a dry disposable razor. Not even if you're in a hurry. Mopping up rivers of blood won't help your time management.

A quick word about your **lower arms**. Yes, they're a bit hairy. But aren't everybody's?

You're best off leaving them alone.

Don't believe me?

Well, I conducted a highly scientific piece of research on Twitter.

> **@hayleywrites:** Quick Research Survey.
> Women: shaving your forearms? YES or NO?
> Thank you x

Within seconds the response from the world was this:

> **@hayleywrites** NO NO NO NO NO. :)

And that was a unanimous verdict.

OK. Moving south.

Pubic hair

. . . is nothing to be ashamed of. Please don't read anything into that comparatively small heading. I mean . . . do you **really** want to see . . .

. . . written any bigger?

Didn't think so.

Well, here's the thing. Do these need to be a top priority? In case you haven't noticed, your pubes are in a very private and protected place. It's a reasonable guess that **only you** have full knowledge of what's occurring pube-wise. And your skin down there is especially sensitive.

So why prune your pubes unnecessarily?

However, if it's growing like Japanese knotweed and looks like a furry animal trying to escape from your swimsuit, and you want to do something about it, you can take the action outlined on the next page.

HOW TO PERFORM A BIKINI-LINE TRIM

You will need:

A pair of small, clean scissors. Nail scissors will do the job perfectly. Whichever scissors you use, put them aside and think of them as your **pube scissors.**

A compact hand mirror.

Somewhere that's easy to clean. Maybe stand in a dry shower. Or sit on or stand next to the toilet. This will make cleaning up those stray pubes much easier.

Method:

The key rule to remember is this:

Trim dry. Shave wet.

It's easy. Trim your dry bush with the clean scissors—but not so closely that you are in any danger of cutting yourself.

Using the compact mirror to see, trim back any hair that's threatening to tuft out of your bikini bottoms.

Rinse the shower or flush the toilet, wash your scissors, and away you go.

If you want to remove any random dark hairs creeping along your inner thigh or up towards your belly button, shave them off. Follow the steps to **wet shaving**—carefully.

In case you were wondering . . .

You may have heard of people getting **a Brazilian**. No mystery. They're just talking about a **pubic hairdo** that involves **waxing** themselves **pretty much bald** or **completely bald**. It's famously painful.

But most women just do the bikini-line trim, if anything. According to the internet, anyway. I really can't claim to have asked any of them.

But waxing and shaving and bleaching and Brazilians are all just mere details. The only thing that **really matters** is this:

> Keep your lady bits fresh
> and clean. This is just basic
> health and hygiene.

Everything else is a matter of preference.

It's up to you, isn't it? What you do with your pubes (and all the other hair on you)?

IT SURE IS!
AND IT ALWAYS
WILL BE, GIRL.

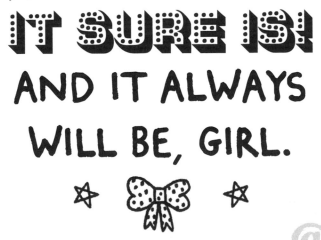

Chapter 7

MATTERS OF THE HEART

It all starts with one little random thought . . .

I really like you.

Which quickly grows into . . .

OH WOW, I LIKE YOU!

And before you know it, **all other thoughts** are squashed right out of your brain.

Yep. Welcome to the world of the **Teen Crush.**

Or perhaps you prefer to call it

LOVE SICKNESS

or **THE HOTS**   or   *Crushasaurus Rex*

or

PLAIN LUST.

Whatever you call it, it's INTENSE.
It's also completely normal, of course. (Despite being thought of as a teen thing, a crush is something anyone can get on anyone else at any time in their life.)

Because human beings like each other.

Which is **great** when you like someone who likes you back. But potentially **very stressful** when the person you have a crush on:

→ • has no idea you're alive.
- has absolutely no idea how you feel about them.
- knows how you feel and . . . just . . . laughs.
- is going out with your best friend.
- is going out with your sister.
- is going out with anyone who isn't you.
- is your cute geography teacher.
- is *any* teacher whatsoever.
- is your best friend.
- is actually just a sad poster on your bedroom wall.

This pretty much means that most of the world's population is going to experience some sort of crush-related stress at some point. And usually crush-related stress **is** a teen thing. Because teens tend to like each other a whole lot. Blame those pesky head-messing hormones again.

FYI, LIKING YOUR TEACHER

. . . is a **monumental** waste of time. Even if you're in high school. According to **Federal Sexual Offense Laws**, any teacher who has any romantic involvement with a student is **abusing a position of trust**. And this means he or she will most likely end up in prison. So if you have a crush on your teacher, just forget it. **Nothing is ever going to happen**. Not unless your teacher is a sketchy pervert. And who the heck wants to go out with a sketchy pervert?

So teachers are a **total turnoff**. Forget them. Now let's address another of those stressful crushes:

Liking your best friend

Maybe your best friend is a boy? And you have secret yearnings of hot lust for him? Yep, it's a tricky dilemma. Say nothing and you might be his best friend forever—when actually you'd much rather be his girlfriend / partner / soulmate / wife [delete as appropriate]. But let him know how you feel and there's the risk that he'll say:

Sorry, but now that I'm aware you harbor these romantic feelings for me that I don't return, I feel a bit weird about us hanging out together.

It's a stressful position for any best friend to find herself in. But what if you're going through all this and the BFF you have a crush on is a *girl*? Just like you.

Yes, it happens—and probably a lot more than anyone ever admits. If you don't believe me, have a quick look through the problem pages of a few teen-girl magazines. I can pretty much guarantee that you won't have to look through them for long before you find a letter from someone who is freaking out over **exactly** this predicament. If **you** ever find yourself in this position, please don't panic. **You are not a freak.** You're just a little bit in love with your friend. And that's a **lot less weird** than being friends with someone who makes you want to secretly vomit.

But doesn't it make me a Lezzie?

No, it doesn't. It may though, and that's totally fine. If you're wondering, turn the page and check the chart.

But before we go any further, let's be clear about something.

"Lezzie" is a banned word. So is "lesbo," "lesbot," or anything else that is a snarky substitute for the word "**lesbian**."

Some people are tall. Some people aren't. Some people are straight. Some people aren't. That's just life. No snarkiness necessary.

Now let's get back to answering the question.

Liking your best friend doesn't mean you're gay.

In fact, liking **any** girl doesn't mean you're gay. Or even bisexual—which means sexually attracted to both males **and** females. Being a teenager is a rollercoaster ride. Everything feels intense and every day is different. One day you may be obsessed with Ansel Elgort or Justin Bieber. The next day it might be Jennifer Lawrence. The day after that it could be Steve Carrell.*

The teenage brain is young and fresh and all over the place. It isn't ready to be labeled and put in a corner.

Of course, this doesn't solve the problem of **what to do** if you have a crush on your best friend. It's a tricky conundrum. But events can only unfold in so many ways.

Please peruse **The "Ohmygosh, I Like My Female Friend" Flowchart.**

(By the way, this chart works just as well if your best friend is a boy. Because a crush is a crush. If he's a boy, just stick to the gray areas. If she's a girl, you can use the white areas too.)

---

* This is known as a Weird Crush. If we're honest with ourselves, we all have the occasional one of these. Me included. Currently, mine is—What?!? Did you actually think I was going to divulge this very personal piece of information??? Oh. OK then. It's the comedian Micky Flanagan.

✱✱✱✱✱✱✱ ✱✱

The "Ohmygosh, I Like My

You have two options:

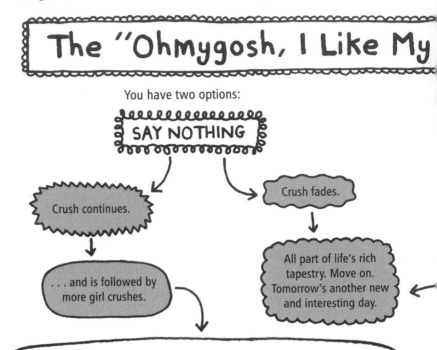

SAY NOTHING

Crush continues.

Crush fades.

. . . and is followed by more girl crushes.

All part of life's rich tapestry. Move on. Tomorrow's another new and interesting day.

So maybe you *are* gay. If so, you'll probably know. Many people who identify themselves as gay are aware of this fact from a fairly young age—sometimes even preadolescence. It's just part of the process of discovering who you are. The only difficult thing about it is the possibility of getting a bad and homophobic reaction from other people. But attitudes are changing fast. In many—but not enough—countries around the world, gay couples can get married just the same as straight couples can. And they can adopt children just like straight couples can. This shift in attitude is long overdue.

There have always been gay people. Always. Leonardo da Vinci was gay. So was the Emperor Hadrian—that Roman guy with the big wall. It's harder to name famous gay women from a long time ago because, as we've already seen, ancient history isn't really about women.

Remember, a gay crush, a gay kiss . . . even a gay relationship . . . still doesn't mean you **are** gay. Or bisexual. I hate to use the expression *maybe it's just a phase . . .* but . . .

maybe it's just a phase. Who knows?

All that really matters is that **the world is not going to end**. For more information and advice on this subject, have a look at www.glaad.org.

Female Friend" Flowchart

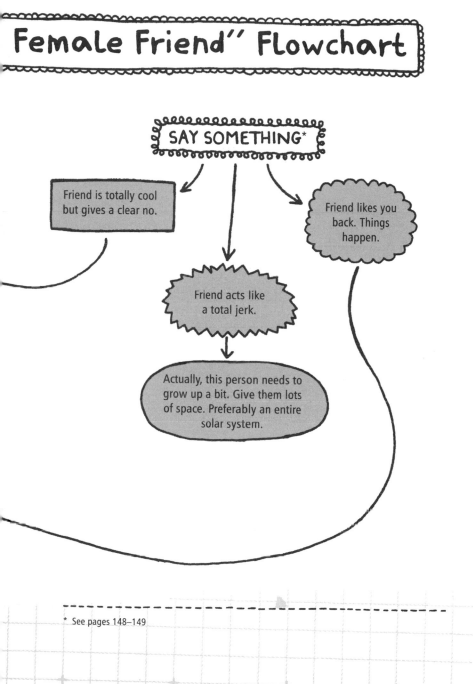

SAY SOMETHING*

Friend is totally cool but gives a clear no.

Friend likes you back. Things happen.

Friend acts like a total jerk.

Actually, this person needs to grow up a bit. Give them lots of space. Preferably an entire solar system.

* See pages 148–149

I'm sure I don't need to say this but I'm going to anyway. If you ever find yourself on the **receiving end** of any unwanted crush—from a boy **or** a girl—**please don't be a jerk.**

Being liked by anyone is a **massive compliment.** Somebody thinks you're lovely. So keep on being lovely, and **gently** and **clearly** let that person know that you're very flattered but you're not the right person for them. A polite but clear **no** is the only acceptable response.

End of drama.

Now to something less complicated:

Liking a face on a poster

. . . is standard practice. Everyone does this for a while. It only gets weird if you **never ever** get over it. And bombard that famous face on your poster with hundreds of emails. And track down their home address so you can shower them with small fluffy gifts. And get their face printed on your pillow / mug / cushion / T-shirt / etc. If this happens, **you've crossed a line.**

STOP IT.

But otherwise, liking famous people is totally harmless and shouldn't cause you any sort of stress at all. In fact, this sort of crush is low risk. You're never going to get dumped, your school work isn't going to suffer, and when you're bored, you can toss him aside. Or her. Quite literally.

Low risk. But low on excitement too.

And now we arrive at the rather big subject of . . .

Have I gone boy crazy?

It's weird. Cast your mind back to when you were a little girl. What were your feelings regarding little boys? It's a generalization, of course, but little boys tend to make little girls feel a bit sick. Because little boys are way too loud. They fart and think it's funny. There are sometimes thick green snot issues . . .

It's fair to say that, in elementary school, there are few things more upsetting than when your teacher says . . .

But in middle school, something changes. Chatting about boys becomes a national pastime. Many girls get completely obsessed. **Not all.**

All different, remember?

Look at the checklist below to find out how you may stand.

AM I BOY CRAZY?		
Typical Behavioral Symptoms	Yes, I have done this.	NO Way!
Constantly wondering if you will EVER have a boyfriend.	☐	☐
Adding a sexy boy's last name onto your first name and then writing it down somewhere. Like this: **Hayley Claflin**	☐	☐
Writing a sonnet (that's a love poem with fourteen lines, thank you very much) or **any other kind of poem** about a boy you like. Or writing a story. About you and him. Getting together.	☐	☐
Writing a letter you will never ever send to the boy of your dreams.	☐	☐
Losing all appetite / power of speech / sensible brain activity whenever a **certain someone** is in earshot / eyesight.	☐	☐
Sniffing all the male deodorants in the supermarket to see which one HE wears.	☐	☐
Staying on the bus past your stop just because HE'S SITTING ON THAT SEAT OVER THERE.	☐	☐
Doing weird little math calculations to find out the **exact percentage** of how much YOU and HIM love each other.	☐	☐
Writing stuff like this: Hayley + Sam 2 gether 4 ever 2 luv 1 another 4 years 2 come + never 2 part.	☐	☐

The Scientific Results

No checks = No. You've not lost your mind at all. This might mean:

i) You are extremely cool and at one with yourself.

ii) This phase of your life is yet to come.

iii) Boys aren't your bag.

Either way, it's all cool. Everyone is different.

One check = Yes. You are displaying definite symptoms of **boy infatuation**.

Two to seven checks = Yes. Your brain is **boy-infested jelly**.

Eight to nine checks = Cool your jets, sister.

So, you have a **crush** on a boy.

What are you going to do about it?

Well, you may as well refer back to **The "Ohmygosh, I Like My Female Friend" Flowchart.** Yes, the same chart works for liking boys too. Because a crush is a crush. It's the same weird mix of joy and agony **whomever** you like. You are still left with those same two major options:

If you want him to like you back, you may want to let him know. He's a boy. Not a mind reader.

So let's explore the proactive possibilities a little further.

SAY SOMETHING

VIA STEALTH METHODS

Start LIKING all his comments on Facebook. Build up to leaving actual comments. Then flirt virtually.

Pros: . . . are far out-weighed by the . . .

Cons: He might think you're a Facebook stalker. Or he might be really different online from how he is in real life. Or he isn't **actually** who you think he is at all but, instead, an overweight old Texan called Randy Pervberger.

Join the same track and field, chess club, chemistry club, math club, band. ANYTHING that might get his attention.

Pros: It gets you on his radar.

Cons: But is it honest? (I actually tried this approach in college. I went to lectures for a whole year just to sit next to a guy named Philip. Then he asked me out and took me up a mountain to build a farm wall out of big stones.)

Use your friend as a "middleman." You know the thing: "My friend thinks you're cute."

Pros: Low on risk. If he says no, you can always say it was a dare.

Cons: Lacks sophistication. Let's be honest, this is a bit preschool. And there's the danger that any future boy you ask out will think that it's just another dare.

DIRECTLY TO HIS FACE

Pros: Win or lose, you are acting like a true lioness. If he's got any sense, he'll respect that—and so will his friends.

Cons: Scary. Takes some courage.

A boy is not an alien. Just TALK to him. 🪐

Telling someone that you like them is a **nice** thing. So—unless he's a total idiot—he'll be flattered at the very least. And lots of boys are just as freaked out by this whole dating process as girls are. Don't forget, they are going through puberty too. One of the lovely high school boys in my Student Focus Group said this:

There's nothing worse than people who don't act like themselves.

That's right. Imagine. You could spend **a whole year** of your life doing something that doesn't really interest you just to win the attention of someone **you don't have anything in common with**. How utterly pointless is that?

So listen to what the boy says and ➡️

JUST BE YOURSELF!

FYI, another one of my helpful high school boys said this:

I'd Quite like it if a girl asked me out.

See? What did I tell you?

So let's take this a little further. You've let him know you like him and it turns out that he likes you back.

BOOM!

What happens next?

The date

Yes. You're going to go on a date with him. This is fantastically exciting but it's also **totally mind-boggling** at the same time. Unless you're cooler than Cleopatra, the inside of your head will be something like this:

Recognize those thoughts?

OK, just relax. Put some music on while you're getting ready. Calm yourself down a bit. Now let's deal with these concerns in order of importance. Most essential first.

No. And if he expects you to do **anything** you aren't comfortable doing, just say, "I'm not ready for that." Be clear. Be cool. He'll understand. He'll probably even feel like a great big idiot and apologize. And if he **doesn't** understand and starts acting like a total jerk, then he's not a boy you want to be going out with. Sadly, he **is** a **Total Jerk**. Ditch him.

Clothes. The key thing is to wear something that makes you feel **comfortable** and **confident**. If you feel nice, you'll have a better time. But if you're constantly tugging on the hemline of your dress to check that it hasn't ridden up over your butt cheeks, you'll probably start to feel a bit uptight. And if you're not relaxed, he won't be either. Why do that to yourself?

Also, it's worth remembering that fancy word we discussed earlier:

SEMIOTICS.

You are a book that can be read. And your clothes are the words. What have you got in your wardrobe that best says . . .

It's tricky, isn't it? If it helps, it's tricky for everyone. Boys included. And they usually end up wearing their jeans and sneakers anyway. By the way, there's absolutely no reason why **you** shouldn't do the same if you feel nice in them. And they're clean.

According to my Student Focus Group, it's a really good idea to go somewhere where you've got **something to do.** Males and females all agreed on this. Going somewhere where you'll be entertained takes the pressure off both of you and reduces the possibility of . . .

awkward

silences.

You don't want those. Awkward silences can make your dream date drag on like a detention.

The Student Focus Group suggested the **movies** as an ideal place to go on a first date. It makes sense too.

You get to:

 Sit next to him for ages.

 Hold his hand.

 See a film.

❤ Dodge the dilemma of what to talk about.

Be sure to steer him toward a seat NOT in the back row.
According to the boys I spoke to, any girl who is happy to sit in the back
row is sending out the following signal:

"Let's do sexy things!"

This might seem massively unfair. Perhaps you just love sitting right
at the very back. All I'm saying is that this is a situation where
misunderstanding and awkwardness can **very easily** be avoided.
Sit somewhere else.

Other first date suggestions were the bowling alley or—if you live near
the coast—a visit to the beach. You could also go for a walk in a park—
in which case, make sure it's during daylight hours. Parks after dark are
super sketchy no matter how old you are.

How much money will I need?

Exactly the same amount as you'd take if you
were going out with the girls. This idea that the
male should pay for everything is as prehistoric
as the idea that girls were born to do the dishes.
If he insists on treating you—**great**! Next time,
maybe you should treat *him*.

I doubt it! **He likes you!** He wants to spend time with you. Find out what his interests are. Talk to him about music or TV or things that make you feel happy. Like snow days. Or squirrels on the fence. Or spotting a dog poking his nose out of a car window. Who's not going to smile at chatter like that?

But, crucially . . .

Yes, I know I've made this point already.
But your date needs to like **you**. Not plastic you.

You won't be. Not unless you find him gross. Kissing someone you genuinely like comes very naturally. In fact, it's **EASY.**

Don't believe me? Pucker up and follow these four simple steps . . . ⫸⟶

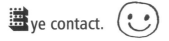 ye contact. :)

 little "we're soooo going to kiss now" smile.

Slow movement of your face toward his.

Yay! Lip contact.

Describing a good kiss is difficult. But it's all about **lip action.**
Your lips should be having a flirty tussle with his.

Approaches you might want to avoid:

1. The Super-Glue Your Mouth to His Method.

2. Saliva Face Wash.

3. Too Much Tongue.

One quick word about **hickeys.**

Y U C k.

They suck. OK, so that's just my opinion, obviously. But think about it. It's
a big old bruise. A bruise on your **neck.** Hickeys look **hideous.**

Why on earth would anyone want one?

Unless it's to say . . .

Stay classy. Avoid the hickey.

There's still another pre-date panic we haven't dealt with yet. This one:

Do you know that old song?

There's a lot of truth in that. Life doesn't come with a list of guarantees. Sometimes things go perfectly to plan and sometimes they don't. First dates are always a bit of a question mark. You might have a great time. Or you might be bored to tears and quietly decide **never** to go out with him again. If so, be nice about it. You can get your life back **without** resorting to these kinds of shady tactics:

WRONG!

> No offense, but UR not my type. CU around. LOL.

The dignified finish

Whether you've been going out with someone for one week or one year, text dumping is **bad.** It's casual, it's careless, and it lacks class. Just tell him. Properly. And if that sounds scary, write him a letter.

An **actual** letter.

Handwritten!

Old style.

And then write his address on an envelope, put a stamp on it, and mail it to him. This might sound weird but letters are so much better for communicating emotional stuff than coldhearted emails in an inbox. It shows that you've made a special effort to be thoughtful and considerate. Just say something like this . . .

Dear Austin,

Thanks for a lovely afternoon at the movies / bowling alley / beach the other day. I especially enjoyed the part when Darth Vader died / I scored a strike / the seagull stole your ice cream. However, I've been doing a lot of thinking and I really don't want to get into anything serious right now. It's absolutely nothing you've said or done; I just like being single. I do hope we can still be friends though.

All the best,

Hayley

This might sound like something your grandma would write, but, given the circumstances, it's a whole lot safer than signing off with "love . . ."

This is one of the few instances when it's OK to lie.

✳✳✳✳✳✳ ✳✳

WHILE WE'RE ON THE SUBJECT OF ENDING IT . . .

There's no point going out with **anyone** unless you think they're a little bit awesome. Especially when you're a teenager. Teen romance should be sweet and exciting and fun and sparky. If it's a tedious drag, why the heck bother?

Below is a list of VERY BADLY WRONG reasons for calling anyone your boyfriend.

✗ I'm desperate. He'll do.

✗ I felt sorry for him.

✗ I can get closer to his best friend who is **massively** hot.

✗ His dad owns a movie theater. I can get free tickets for all my friends.

✗ It means I'm better at being a girl, doesn't it? If I've got a boyfriend?

No. A lioness doesn't need a boyfriend to make her feel like she's a worthwhile human being.

Of course, there is another scenario. And that is that **you** might want to keep things going, but **he** might not. If he doesn't return your texts, he's clearly not interested. If you've been going out for a while and he tells you he wants to end it, there isn't really anything you can do to change his mind.

NO GIRL SHOULD EVER BEG SOMEONE TO GO OUT WITH HER.

That won't make her more attractive to him. Or to anyone.

Being turned down or dumped is never nice. It's a nasty blow to the ego. Sometimes, it can even feel devastating. But really . . .

It just means you haven't found the right person yet.

And the truth is that very few people **do** find their perfect person while they're still in their teens. That's why it's so important to keep spending plenty of time with your friends. A Best Friend Forever might well turn out to be just that. A forever friend. Whereas a whirlwind romance with that boy in your English class who looks a bit like Ryan Gosling will be yesterday's news when you go to college and meet the guy who looks like Zayn Malik.

This is all well and tragic, but there's still a **third** scenario. This one:

What began as a teen crush will blossom into a beautiful relationship.

Who knows? It could be. *"Que sera, sera . . ."* Remember?

So how do I take flight on the wings of love?

It's impossible to say for sure why some relationships work out and others don't—but a fairly useful recipe is this one:

How to Cook Up a Lasting Romance

You will need:

1 cup of honesty
1 cup of trust
A generous handful of consideration
A good sprinkling of chemistry
A lively teaspoon of humor

Method:

Mix all the ingredients.
Divide into two portions and share.

OK, so maybe that recipe is a little vague—and a **lot** cheesy. Perhaps the Good Girlfriend Test will help . . .

The Good Girlfriend Test

1. **It's your first date. You and Lover Boy have gone to the movies. LB offers to buy a bucket of popcorn for you both to share. Do you say:**

> **A.** Cool. And get a bag of chocolate peanuts too. And some nachos. And an extra large cola, cuz I'm bound to work up a thirst.

> **B.** Oh, thank you! And I hope that this is the start of us sharing many, **many** things together. Including our entire future lives.

> **C.** You like popcorn? It tastes like polystyrene! I can't take you seriously if you **actually** think polystyrene tastes nice.

> **D.** Are you trying to make me fat?

> **E.** That sounds great. Thanks.

2. **It's LB's birthday. Do you get him:**

> **A.** Nothing. Treat him mean, keep him keen.

> **B.** A picture album. Filled with all the photos you've ever taken of him. And your gift is completed by a heart-shaped note explaining that the blank pages at the back will one day be filled with snaps of your wedding and your children and your grandchildren and your great-grandchildren.

C. Something decent to wear. Because **somebody** has to.

D. A mobile phone. It's expensive but it's worth it. Cuz you've downloaded an app called THE BOYFRIEND TRACKING DEVICE so you can see where he is ALL THE TIME.

E. A card. And movie tickets—a smiling nod of recognition to that first sweet date.

3. It's your birthday. LB gives you a CD of special songs that he's burned for you himself. And he invites you over to his house. He's cooked you lasagna and a chocolate birthday cake. Do you say:

A. Where's my **actual** present?

B. Thank you so much. These are the songs we will dance to at our wedding. And all our guests will eat lasagna and chocolate cake.

C. I'm really going to have to do something about your tragic taste in music. The lasagna and chocolate cake are fine though.

D. What are you after? Are you inviting me to your house just to tell me I'm dumped?

E. That's really sweet. Thanks. I'll burn a CD of songs for you too.

4. LB's good-looking friend corners you at a house party and says, "You should be going out with me— not him." Do you:

A. Kiss him. Then tell him you're confused. Then tell him to keep his big blabby mouth shut.

B. Show him the gold ring drawn in felt-tip pen on the third finger of your left hand and say, "I am already married. This felt-tip ring symbolizes the gold and diamond-encrusted ring that *[insert LB's name]* will one day buy me. Our hearts and souls are connected and no one—I repeat **no one**—will ever pull us apart."

C. Go and tell LB. But also tell him it was **kind of sexy** and he really needs to **up his game** if he wants to keep you.

D. Realize **immediately** that it's an evil trap. LB and his best friend are obviously in cahoots to check out how faithful you are. Or maybe LB's friend is just trying to stop you from noticing that LB has disappeared somewhere with **your** best friend.
OH MY GODDDDDD!

E. Just tell his sleazy friend to forget it.

5. LB tells you he's going away to England for a month in the summer with his soccer team. Do you:

    A. Rub your hands together in delight. While the cat's away . . .

    B. Wail. Throw yourself onto the ground. Hug his legs. Wail louder. Tell him **you will die** if he leaves you.

    C. Tell him he can have either you **or** the soccer team. Not both. It's decision time.

    D. Sense there's something going on. You can sniff a lie a mile away. He just wants to be rid of you, doesn't he? He's seeing someone else, isn't he?

    E. Feel a bit sad. But then it's only for a month, isn't it? And a soccer tour to England sounds like an amazing experience. And he said he'd bring you back a present . . .

SO HOW DID YOU DO?

Mostly As: Ooops. Looks like you're in it for what you can get. Romance is about the feelings of **two people**. At the moment, it looks like you're only interested in yourself.

Mostly Bs: Are you human or are you Klingon? **Relax.** You're only young. Time is on your side. Unless you find someone as clingy as you are, you're going to frighten everyone away.

Mostly Cs: You are displaying all the signs of harboring this hugely unhelpful thought:

I like you—now *change*.

A relationship will only work if **you** are allowed to be yourself and you allow your partner to be *him*self. (Or herself. Straight or gay, we all need space to be our own person.)

Mostly Ds: Gosh. You are one **suspicious girl**! You must trust and believe in people or life becomes impossible.*

Mostly Es: Yes. You're doing all right. Good going, girl!

But let's go back to a bit of old nonsense mentioned in Question 2.

TREAT THEM MEAN, KEEP THEM KEEN.

Really? Really? How does that work? We aren't mean to our friends, are we? If we were, we'd probably end up sitting home alone. **Boyfriends are human beings too.** Treat them mean and it just means that . . . well . . . you're mean. And who—other than a tragic desperado—wants to go out with someone who is mean?

A much better bit of old nonsense is this:

Don't give away the farm just to sell a few eggs.

---

* I stole this bit of wisdom from Anton Chekhov. He was a very intense Russian writer who lived from 1860 to 1904. He was totally right about the trust thing.

You've got your whole life ahead of you. There's no need to rush into anything. You like this boy and he likes you. So don't let him squeeze your turnips and sow his wild oats in your fertile land just as a way of keeping him interested.

Because once that's done, what more have you got to stop him from getting bored?

Know what I'm saying?

And that brings us very conveniently to one small word I haven't yet mentioned.

Sex

There's a reason this hasn't been mentioned until now. And it's this:

Being someone's girlfriend doesn't mean you MUST be having sex.

Especially when you're a teenager.

In fact, according to the law, you shouldn't be. Not unless you and your partner have **both** reached the age of consent.* And this is the same for everyone. Straight or gay.

---

* Remember, this varies from sixteen to eighteen years old depending on which US state you live in.

And just in case there's any confusion. Sex doesn't **just** mean penises in vaginas—or **penetrative sex,** as it's more properly known. It also means **oral sex** (doing it with the mouth) and **mutual masturbation**—also known as heavy petting,* fingering, and hand jobs.

Think of it this way: **Wherever there's an underage person in a sexual situation, there's also** *potentially* **someone else in a whole heap of trouble. Even if that other person is underage too!**

Of course, plenty of teens are still going to have sex. Especially the heavy petting / fingering / hand job sort. You know it. I know it. Everyone knows it. And usually no one gets into any trouble at all. So does that mean that the **age of consent laws** are a big fat waste of time? And patronizing? And unfair?

No, it doesn't. Because they're there to **protect you.**

If anyone ever starts whining like this . . .

> What kind of a wicked, heartless girlfriend are you if you won't let me have sex with you?

*. . . but only by adults who are too embarrassed to use the more direct teen-favored terms of "fingering" and "hand job." To be honest, none of these expressions are great. I wouldn't advise using any of them out loud. But "heavy petting" is the worst somehow. It's down there on the same level of awfulness as "breast buds."

You are well within your legal rights to reply . . .

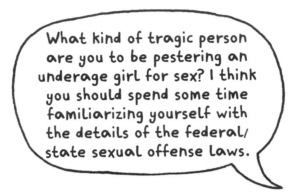

> What kind of tragic person are you to be pestering an underage girl for sex? I think you should spend some time familiarizing yourself with the details of the federal/state sexual offense laws.

And then draw a line through that relationship. **Anyone who pesters anyone else for sex isn't a good catch.**

When you're under the age of consent, having a boyfriend and having sex **don't** necessarily belong on the same page. In fact, sex is a whole other chapter.

Chapter 8

SEX: ON A NEED TO KNOW BASIS

JUST GOOD STUFF

✳✳✳✳✳✳ ✳✳

DISCLAIMER

This chapter is unlikely to turn you on.

Sorry, not sorry—it's just not that sort of book.

You won't find any erotic, thrusting details of what happens when people are **doing it**. Or a saucy selection of spine-tingling sex tips for turned-on teens. Or great big extended descriptions of the **ins** and **outs** of what sex feels like. There's none of that here. Because **real** sex—**not** the fantasy sort that fills the pages of steamy paperbacks—is a very intimate and personal experience. It's something that nature lets you discover for yourself.

You'll know what to do when the moment arrives.

But if—after reading this chapter—you still have questions about **doing it**, go to youngwomenshealth.org. They may not be able to give you all the answers but they will be able to offer you excellent advice.

Classic nonpology!

Let's start with some statistics.

According to the good folks at the global children's charity UNICEF, the United States tops the table for the number of teenage girls giving birth in a "rich" country.*

The UK is right behind them.

There are quite a lot of teen moms in Hungary, Poland, and Iceland too.

But that's only part of the picture. The United States and the UK also have very high rates of teen abortion. So do Sweden, Estonia, and France.**

Sometimes being at the top of the charts isn't that great.

So let's remind ourselves of something that sometimes gets forgotten in the heat of the moment.

If you *do it*,

you could end up

PREGNANT.

Unless you take very careful precautions, of course. We'll talk more about those a bit later.

---

* This information has been taken from a 2013 UNICEF report called "Child Well-Being in Rich Countries." The address for UNICEF's excellent website is www.unicef.org.
** And this information comes from a study by the Guttmacher Institute. This is an organization that aims to improve the sexual and reproductive health of all the people of the world. That sounds like a good aim!

The second thing to say is this:

You'll know if you are ready.
You will know.

There'll be **no doubts** in your head at all. Just good stuff. And you'll feel totally **safe** and **happy** about the person you are with. When it comes to sex . . .

THERE'S NO SUCH THING AS A BLURRED LINE.

Either you're absolutely 100% up for it or you're not. Of course, this is equally true of your partner. Neither of you should need any persuasion.

If, on the other hand, you've got a few worries wiggling about in the back of your mind—or even just **one** worry—then you aren't ready. In which case, **don't do it**. Because you won't enjoy it. And if you don't enjoy it, the experience will rank somewhere on a rating between disappointing and disastrous. It definitely won't be sexy—which is a shame because sexy is **exactly** what sex is supposed to be.

So if things seem to be heading in a certain direction, take time out to check the contents of your head. If you find any of these thoughts . . .

. . . then . . .

WAIT.

And tell him that either:

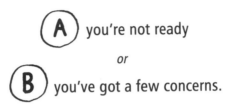

A you're not ready

or

B you've got a few concerns.

If you're not ready to have that kind of intimate conversation, the truth is that you're not ready to have sex with him either.

And there's absolutely nothing wrong with that.

Just hang on for a bit and make your first time a special experience with someone you **really like** in a **double bed** behind a **firmly closed door**. This is **a much better plan** than doing it under a table at a house party. Or in a gross underpass that smells of dog pee. Or anyplace where your little brother or sister might overhear.

Gosh. This is all getting a bit serious, isn't it? But that's because sex **is** a serious business. Don't get me wrong, done right (meaning, for starters—at the right time, with the right person), it can also be . . .

fun and **FANTASTIC**

and flipping emotional

. . . but it needs a lot of thinking through beforehand. By **both** partners. Because sex is also about **reproduction**. Although, it's only ever **the girl** who has to squeeze a great big melon-headed baby out through a ridiculously tiny hole. Or make that joyless trip to the abortion clinic with her mother.

Always the girl.
Never the boy.

So if you're gonna do it, make sure YOU are being treated with ALL due care and consideration.

And make sure you're happy with every part of the arrangement.

So what's it really all about?

The most simplistic answer is: the survival of the human race. Men and women **need** to have sex in order to create more human beings. To tempt us into action, nature has made the experience extra appealing by inventing sensations like **love** and **lust**.

It's all extremely clever. And it's powered by nature's chemicals again.

It all begins as simply as ABC . . .

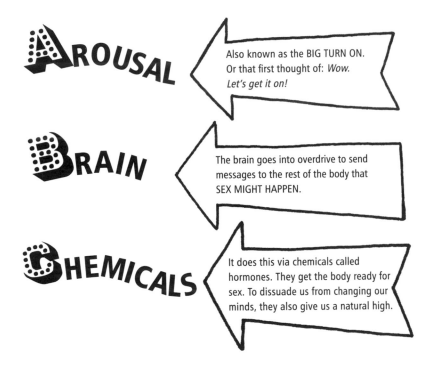

AROUSAL

Also known as the BIG TURN ON. Or that first thought of: *Wow. Let's get it on!*

BRAIN

The brain goes into overdrive to send messages to the rest of the body that SEX MIGHT HAPPEN.

CHEMICALS

It does this via chemicals called hormones. They get the body ready for sex. To dissuade us from changing our minds, they also give us a natural high.

Very often:

Remember, this can be penetrative sex, oral sex, or mutual masturbation. Or just masturbation if the person is a solo operator. (See page 182.)

All this applies equally to males and females. It's also worth noting that despite the fact that it takes a male + a female to make a baby, it doesn't take a male + a female to achieve arousal. A male can get turned on by another male and a female can get turned on by another female. And lone individuals can get turned on all by themselves.

So sex isn't just about making babies. It's about having a very nice time too.

And for girls, the center of all the excitement is downstairs in the vagina department. In case you've never picked up a mirror and made a thorough inspection of your property, it's all arranged something like this:

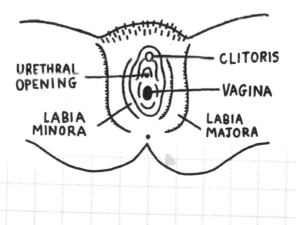

✳✳✳✳✳✳ ✳✳

If ever there was an **ON** button, the clitoris is it. Only females have them. The clitoris is **extremely sensitive** and has no known use whatsoever—other than to feel supersexyohmygosh when touched. If this supersexyohmygosh feeling reaches a toe-tingling point of **WOWWW**, the woman has reached sexual climax—or **orgasm**. This doesn't always happen—and it's much less likely to if the important button hasn't been properly "pressed."

PUSHING YOUR OWN BUTTONS

DO NOT DISTURB

Males have no qualms about pushing their own buttons. In fact, teenage boys and masturbation go together pretty much hand in . . . um . . . I mean . . . hand **on** . . . I think you get my drift.

But for some reason, **female masturbation** isn't something that gets spoken about very often.

While it's definitely **not** a good topic for the dinner table, **there is absolutely nothing wrong with masturbation**. And logistically, all that's needed are your own clean hands and a relaxing environment where you **definitely won't be disturbed.** Like your bedroom or the bathroom. Pushing your own buttons is actually a good way to get to know your body and what feels nice. And it's probably the safest kind of sex there is.

But at some point in your life, there's likely to be a special someone who is all too happy to push those buttons for you. Whoever it is, they'll want you to do the same for them. If it's a guy, his sex bits will look like this:

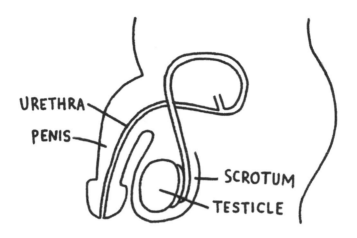

If the clitoris is the female **ON** switch—then the penis is surely the male **POWER** button. Or perhaps we should call it a knob. When the male is aroused, his penis will stiffen and swell. If he stays aroused, his penis will become fully erect.

Let's leave this interesting image and switch our minds to something else.

Ask yourself this question:

The answer to that may well be something like this:

> # HELL YEAH.
> ## In fact, I want twins.
> I've already decided they'll be called Dakota and Montana and I'm going to dress them from head to toe in Gucci Baby and they'll be super adorable! But, obviously, I want to get my degree in Chemical Engineering first.

But I'm not talking about **after** you've been to college or traveled around the world or gotten married or moved in with your boyfriend or been working for a few years or reached a point in your life where you feel all hunky-dory and settled—I'm talking about **right now.**

While you're still a teenager—living at home with your parents and going to school every day.

If your answer is still YES, think VERY HARD.

You'd probably miss out on

HUGE CHUNKS
OF YOUR EDUCATION
and

tons of interesting career opportunities

and

CAREFREE
NIGHTS OUT

and

money to spend on yourself

but most of all you'd miss out on **SLEEP.**

And yes, you'd gain an amazing
little baby—but that's a helluva
lot of responsibility to take on
before you've barely been let
loose on the world yourself.

There's no big rush. Fertility rates in women don't decline until they're well into their thirties. Chill out. Get yourself a pet rabbit instead.

But you probably have **no flipping intention** of becoming the only teen mom in your school—in which case, it's easy: Either **don't** have penetrative sex **or** make sure he is wearing a **condom**. Every single time you do it.

Condoms are clever little things.

They fulfill two very important functions.

 They stop semen from entering the vagina and playing an exciting game called *Can We Fertilize the Egg?*

 They provide you with evidence that your boyfriend respects you and your body.

It works like this:

The "Why He Should Wear a Condom" Flowchart

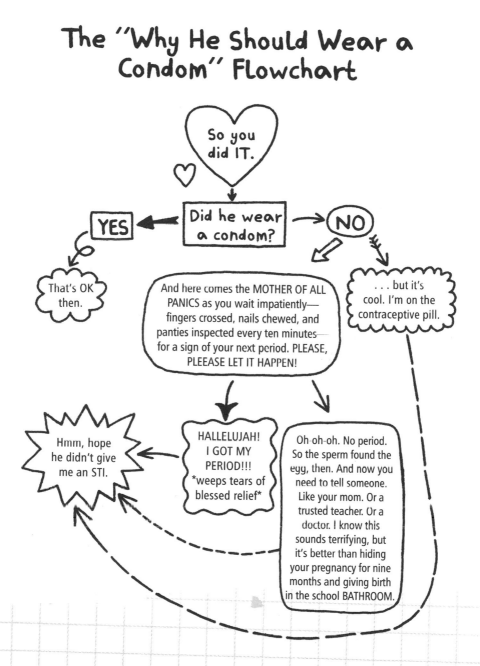

In case this all sounds **way too alarming**, let me just make two things clear.

⇒ Having sex without contraception doesn't mean you **will** get pregnant. But you might.

⇒ Having sex without using a condom doesn't mean you **will** get a sexually transmitted infection. But you might.

Life is stressful enough. Why give yourself this additional worry?

Other types of contraception are available. But the only one that will act as a barrier against sexually transmitted infections is the good old condom. Make sure he wears one. If he's a good sort of boyfriend, he will. End of discussion. But if he says . . .

. . . then I'm afraid that what your boyfriend **actually** needs is a giant-sized condom he can climb right into. Because he's behaving like a dick.

Did someone mention the Morning—After Pill?

This is also known as **emergency contraception**. And that's really what it's for—an EMERGENCY. This shouldn't be something you routinely take after you've gotten carried away with your condomless boyfriend.

The Morning-After Pill is taken as soon as possible after you've had sex—which is awkward because it's not very easy to get your hands on. You'll probably need to speak to your doctor or visit a walk-in medical center. Also, it's very strong medication and it's likely to make you feel a bit sick and dizzy. Sort of takes the shine off the fun of the night before, really . . .

Needless to say:

PREVENTION IS ALWAYS BETTER THAN CURE.

. . . Although, in the case of pregnancy, *cure* isn't really the right word at all. Because you aren't actually sick. All that's happened is that your reproductive system has been activated and now the nine-month process of making a baby is underway. So let's start again.

PREVENTION
IS ALWAYS BETTER
THAN TERMINATION.

Remember those statistics? Not all teen pregnancies result in childbirth.

An abortion is medical intervention to end a pregnancy. There are lots of different reasons why any girl or woman might opt for an abortion and it's absolutely her right to do so. It's her body, after all. And bringing a brand-new life into the world is an enormous responsibility and something that any mother will be aware of for the rest of her life—regardless of whether she keeps her baby or has it adopted. Sometimes, ending a pregnancy may, in fact, be the better option. But it's also a very difficult and upsetting decision for any teenage girl or woman to have to make. Abortions are not nice experiences. They involve either:

A. taking two heavy doses of drugs that force the body into early miscarriage

or

B. a surgical procedure where the unborn baby—or fetus—is vacuumed out.

Make sure he wears a condom.

The
CONTRACEPTIVE
PILL

Another popular form of contraception is the Pill. Some males like it because it means they can have sex without the kerfuffle of using a condom. Girls like it for the exact same reason **and** because it means they'll have much lighter periods. In fact, if a girl regularly has very painful periods, her doctor may even suggest that she goes "on the Pill"—regardless of whether she is sexually active or not. This is great—but any girl who is sexually active and on the Pill needs to be aware of two factors:

1. The Pill must be taken **exactly** as prescribed. If you're forgetful and miss a pill here and skip a pill there, you may as well be swallowing Smarties. **The Pill only works as a reliable form of birth control if it's taken properly.**

2. The Pill prevents pregnancy. It does **not** prevent the spread of sexually transmitted infections.

Some light relief

This chapter needs to chill out a bit. Let's have a fun coffee break and play a game. Here's what you have to do. Five teenage couples have been up to all sorts of shenanigans on a Saturday night. But now one girl is panicking with a tadpole-sized baby in her belly . . .

From the clues, can you figure out:

Who is going out with whom?

What they did?

Where they did it?

What happened next?

And crucially . . .

Who's
the daddy?

Read the clues and mark checks and **X**'s in the chart on page 194 to help you unravel the mystery. Remember, every row and column contains just one check. Like this:

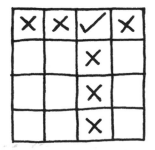

Lorna and her boyfriend —who isn't Jake— couldn't wait to have sex, and didn't think about buying condoms.

Carly's boyfriend's name begins with "B."

Ricky's world changed on a sofa. But in a nice way. Neither he nor his partner has an STI.

Jade wanted to have safe sex so she made sure her boyfriend wore protection; they are still having safe sex.

Clues

Ben had his first ever gay kiss on the sofa while his parents were out. He and his partner are now dating and taking things slowly.

Eddie and his girlfriend—who is not Alisha —had their moment under a table at a friend's party.

Matt and his girlfriend —who is not Carly nor Lorna—had safe sex and continue to do so.

Brad wasn't ready and neither was his girlfriend, so, despite being in the privacy of her bedroom, they decided to wait. And they are still waiting happily.

Alisha couldn't wait to get jiggy with her man, so they ran to the nearest restroom. She thought she was being safe, and she didn't get pregnant, but she caught a nasty STI.

Jake's girlfriend —who is not Jade—is on the Pill, but they didn't do it in his bedroom.

		PARTNERS				
		Eddie	Ricky	Jake	Brad	Matt
PARTNERS	Ben					
	Lorna					
	Alisha					
	Jade					
	Carly					
WHAT THEY DID	Used a condom					
	Decided to wait					
	Sex on the Pill					
	Unprotected sex					
	Made out					
WHERE THEY DID IT	His bedroom					
	Public restroom					
	Sofa					
	At a house party					
	Her bedroom					
WHAT HAPPENED NEXT	Still having safe sex					
	Both have an STI					
	Still happy to wait					
	Pregnant					
	Dating and taking it slowly					

So just who is the daddy?

PARTNERS	WHAT THEY DID	WHERE THEY DID IT	WHAT HAPPENED NEXT

You can find the answers at the back of this book.

Right, let's get back to the serious business of . . .

More sex talk

But first, did I mention that if you choose to have full sexual intercourse, you should make sure he wears a condom?

Well, he absolutely should. Because this will massively reduce any risk of catching a sexually transmitted disease and freaking out about . . .

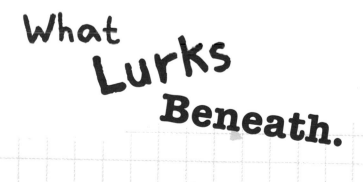

What Lurks Beneath.

STIs (also known as STDs or sexually transmitted diseases) are as glamorous as they sound. They are the much-shared gift that nobody wants. Once you've got one, you'll be itching to get rid of it. Though in truth, they don't always make you itch. Other symptoms include pain when peeing, a rash in your very private place, and smelly vaginal discharges. Sometimes, though, there aren't **any** obvious symptoms at all. This is especially the case for **chlamydia**—which is one of the most common STIs in the United States. It's passed on during sex and often the "giver" and the "recipient" have no idea that anything is wrong. But during all the time it's left undetected and untreated, the chlamydia infection is quietly messing things up inside the body. The most obvious long-term effect is infertility—i.e. not being able to have a baby. If you ever have unprotected sex with someone please see a doctor or visit a Planned Parenthood to be tested for chlamydia and other STIs. Learn more at plannedparenthood.org.

Before you have nightmares and vow **never** to have sex in your entire life, remember that

many people have lots of sex and don't ever encounter any sort of problem.

That may be because they're lucky—just as it's **pretty freaking unlucky** to pick up an infection.* But it's more likely that they're just being a bit **responsible**. Statistically, the fewer sexual partners you have, the less at risk you are of picking up an unwanted souvenir. And the less your partners are at risk from picking up anything from you!

This might sound like a boring piece of fun-sucking propaganda, but it's the mathematical truth.

Also, you're far less likely to ever encounter any problems if he wears a fabulous little thing called a condom. But perhaps I've made that point already . . .

On a **need to know basis,** that's probably enough sex stuff for now. But **in your own good time,** there are plenty of **Very Sexy Things** you can discover for yourself.

---

* If this ever happens—just take a deep breath and go and see your doctor. He or she will give you some medication to treat it. And that's what any infection needs—treatment. You wouldn't ignore a swollen toe or a painful tooth, would you?

It really is worth waiting until you're definitely ready, though. Because it's **always** a million times more fun feeling **utterly electric** and shouting . . .

YES

YES

. . . than it is whispering,

"Oh no."

Chapter 9

BEING
A WOMAN

So there we have it. Being a teenage girl is a unique and memorable and **very special** part of any woman's life. It can be a time of friendship and fun and falling in love and laughing out loud. But it's also a time when we start learning how to live with

gender inequality
and
catty comments
and
periods
and
peer pressure
and
semiotics
and
shaving
and
colossal crushes

. . . and the all-too-frequently forgotten fact that what some boys call

doing
it

. . . is actually a Big Deal.

Being a teenage girl definitely does have its trickier moments. But then again, it's not that simple being a teenage boy either. The truth is that growing up is a strange and challenging time for everyone. And sometimes it might feel like a bit of a struggle. But here's the thing:

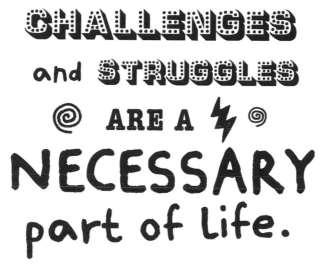

CHALLENGES and STRUGGLES ARE A NECESSARY part of life.

Seriously.

They make us stronger.

And nothing **REALLY SPECIAL** has ever been achieved without a little bit of extra effort.

Have you ever heard the story about the boy and the butterfly? It's just the kind of lame story that you hear in school assembly. But, actually, this story isn't lame. It can't be—because I heard it in a school assembly years ago and I can still remember it. Nobody knows who first told this story because it's so old. So—because it belongs to nobody and everybody—I'm going to tell it to you right now. I've made one or two small adjustments though—just because I can.

The Girl and the Butterfly

One day, a young girl spotted a strange fuzzy object in her garden. It was attached to a leaf on a big plant. The girl ran to get her grandma—who knew everything—and showed her the weird fuzzy thing.

"It's a cocoon," said Grandma—because she knew everything. "Inside it, there's a little caterpillar and when it's ready, it will break its way out of the cocoon and spend the rest of its life as a beautiful butterfly."

The young girl was very interested. Every day, she went into the garden and looked at the cocoon to see if there was any sign of movement.

Not many days later, she saw a big commotion going on inside the fuzzy web of the cocoon. The unhatched butterfly inside was trying to break its way out. But it was struggling. In fact, it appeared to be totally stuck.

The young girl ran into her house and walked back sensibly with a pair of scissors—as you do whenever you're holding scissors. Carefully, she snipped through the cocoon to help the butterfly get out.

A weird creature fell to the ground. It was neither butterfly nor caterpillar. Instead, it was this weird blob with a big body and little shriveled-up wing-things.

"Yuck," said the young girl. And she went to get her grandma.

Her grandma—who knew everything—came out into the garden and looked down at the sorry little thing twitching in the dirt. And then she looked at the scissors in her granddaughter's hand.

"The poor thing is ruined," said Grandma. "It's the struggle to get out of the cocoon that completes the caterpillar's transformation into a butterfly. It's a vital part of the process. The struggle forces fluid out of the caterpillar's body and into its new butterfly wings. This gives the wings all their beautiful colors and makes them strong enough to fly. But now, this weak little thing will never fly. Your kindness was actually cruelty."

And then Grandma stamped hard on the tragic crawly thing and said, "Whereas I'm being cruel to be kind. It's far better to die quickly under my shoe than to be slowly pecked to death by a bird."

From that day on, the young girl never forgot the importance of the occasional struggle.

Let me say it again.

EVERYTHING WORTH HAVING REQUIRES EFFORT

. . . whether it's making lovely friends—and keeping them—or getting fantastic exam results or having a good reputation or passing your driving test.

And some things—like winning an Olympic medal or being a pop star or having a rewarding career doing something you really love—require **a lot** of effort and years and years of determination. Often beginning right **now**. Before you've even finished school. What do you think those test-prep classes are for?

So if some aspects of being a teenage girl feel like a struggle and a nuisance, try to think of it as a **training ground.** How you choose to cope with these teen challenges will help determine what kind of woman you will be one day.

It's up to you.

Do you want to be the sort of woman who gets things done or the sort of woman who can't be bothered to get out of bed?

Do you want to be the sort of woman who has a good job or the sort of woman who gets her mom to write fake sick notes?

Do you want to be the sort of woman who says, "I'll try," or the sort of woman who just shrugs and says, "I can't"?

Do you want to be the sort of woman who is liked and trusted or the sort of woman who talks bad about everyone behind their backs?

Look around you. At school and at home and everywhere you go—all those people milling around are **already** starting to see the sort of woman you might be one day. And that day is not so very far away. If you look in the mirror, you might even catch a glimpse of her yourself.

I've said it before and I'll say it again—**everyone is different.** Some girls like pink things and some girls don't. Some girls like pretty dresses and some girls just won't wear them. Some girls dream of joining the army and some girls sit and dream of their wedding day. And guess what? Some girls dream of doing both. Not everyone dances to the same tune. But so long as we aren't messing up the world or hurting anyone or behaving like shady jerks, does it actually matter?

There's room on this planet for all sorts of people.

Realizing that—and respecting it—is a clear indication that you're growing up. And it means that you can look in the mirror and be perfectly sure that there isn't a shady jerk staring back at you.

So is being a woman very different from being a girl?

Yes and no. You'll probably feel much the same. You'll probably love the same films and the same music and the same books and the same sort of clothes that you've always loved. You may even have some of the same friends. But as you get older, there'll be moments when you definitely feel that something has shifted. Like when you get your first real job. Or when you leave home for the first time and live away from your family. Or when you sit down with a calculator and start figuring out whether you can **actually** afford your cell phone . . .

That something is called **responsibility**.

It will shift from your parents' shoulders to yours. And then you'll be responsible for yourself.

And that really does feel **great** because it means you can make all your own decisions and go wherever you want and do whatever you want and eat whatever you like and dress however you want to dress and live with your friends or your boyfriend or your girlfriend or your pet dog or your house rabbit and stay up all night watching movies and play your music at the loudest volume and put your favorite posters in the best position on your living room wall.

But there'll still be challenges.

Because there are more than **seven billion** people on this planet. The world doesn't owe us anything. In these days of celebrity culture and reality TV, it's easy to forget this. It's easy to think that good things will just miraculously happen to us. They probably won't.*

You have to make the good things happen for yourself by working really hard.

* Harsh, I know. But just like Grandma, I'm being cruel to be kind.

And that's the same for everyone.

But because we're still all living in a world dominated by men, it's **especially** true for girls.

Being a woman involves a boatload of effort. You may well find yourself trying really hard to juggle lots of roles. Perhaps you'll try to be a trusted friend and a thoughtful daughter and a loving partner and a devoted mother and a go-getting professional.

Or perhaps you'll end up doing something entirely different. Perhaps you **won't want** to be anybody's partner. And perhaps you'll never be anyone's mother. Perhaps you'll devote your life to God or discovering a cure for the common cold or perhaps you'll bike around the world or sit on your bottom all day and write books. All these things require a boatload of effort too. Perhaps two boats. Because a few people will look at you sideways and wonder what on earth you are doing with your life.

All you can do is try your best.

GIVE EVERYTHING YOUR BEST SHOT.

And if you start doing that now, you can bet your life that
being a woman will be something **YOU** are

Helpful Websites and Stuff

Fun and Awesomeness
- www.amysmartgirls.com
- www.rookiemag.com
- www.amightygirl.com
- www.girlslife.com
- www.engineergirl.org

Bullying and Abuse
- www.stopbullying.gov
- www.nobullying.com

Physical and Mental Health
- www.girlshealth.gov
- www.teenmentalhealth.org

Sex and Gender
- www.sexetc.org
- www.plannedparenthood.org/teens
- www.advocatesforyouth.org/topics-issues/glbtq/606
- www.itgetsbetter.org

To talk to someone on the phone:
- Childhelp National Child Abuse Hotline 1-800-422-4453
- National Suicide Prevention Lifeline 1-800-273-8255
- Substance Abuse National Helpline 1-500-622-4357
- Teen Line (to talk to teen volunteers)
  1-800-TLC-TEEN (6:00–10:00pm PST) or
  text TEEN to 839863 (5:30–9:30pm PST)

And here's the solution to that puzzle.

PARTNERS	WHAT THEY DID...	WHERE THEY DID IT...	WHAT HAPPENED AFTER...
Matt + Jade	Used a condom	His bedroom	Still having safe sex
Jake + Alisha	Sex on the Pill	Public restroom	Both have an STI
Brad + Carly	Decided to wait	Her bedroom	Still happy to wait
Eddie + Lorna	Unprotected sex	At a house party	Pregnant
Ricky + Ben	Made out	Sofa	Dating & taking it slowly

. . . which means that Eddie is TOTALLY the daddy. Well done if you figured it out!

Thank Yous

I couldn't have written this without talking to loads of people. And asking them quite a lot of personal questions. Sometimes they answered and sometimes they just gave me a funny look.

Anyway, thank you to my niece—Emma Long—who knows far more about eyebrows than I ever will. And also to my friend, Donna Hansell, who told me all about how to walk in high heels, designed the "Who's the Daddy?" quiz, and told me when she thought I was being too frank. Thanks to Professor Susan Basow of Lafayette College, Pennsylvania, who kindly let me use her words in this book. And also to my Student Focus Group—a.k.a. the Very Helpful Students at Paston College, Norfolk, who were happy to chip in with their ideas and opinions, and were the best cheerleaders ever. The future of Norfolk is in safe hands.

Thanks to my mum for helping me get through my teenage years alive. Thanks to my husband—Graham—for absolutely everything. Thanks to Jenny Jacoby and all the lovely people at Hot Key Books and thanks as well to Joanna Devereux and Tim Bates at Pollinger Literary Agency. Finally, I'm enormously grateful to my fellow Norwich-based Ipswichian Gemma Correll for her fab illustrations—and also to James Dawson, who wrote the wonderful *Being a Boy* and provided the perfect pathway for me to follow.

But most of all, thanks to you for reading it all. ✖

About the Author

Hayley Long began writing teen fiction while working as an English teacher in Cardiff. Her first teen novel, *Lottie Biggs Is (Not) Mad* was awarded the White Raven label for outstanding children's literature by the International Youth Library. Since then, her fingers haven't stopped typing. Hayley has been a winner of the Essex Book Award, and *What's Up with Jody Barton?* was short-listed for a Costa Book Award. Hayley has also enjoyed the razzle-dazzle of being a Queen of Teen nominee. *Being a Girl* is Hayley's first nonfiction title, and she's also working on her next novel.

Follow Hayley on Facebook at
www.facebook.com/
HayleyLongAuthor
or on Twitter: @hayleywrites

About the Illustrator

Illustrator Gemma Correll is one of the few people in the universe who has managed to turn her love of pugs into a lucrative career. She has exhibited all over the world; in China, the US, and Europe, and was the recipient of a Young Guns award from the Art Directors Club of New York in 2010. She's a serial punner with a crush on all things cartoony, and studied graphic design in Norwich. Her favorite color is turquoise, her star sign is Aquarius, and her favorite word is Albuquerque, just in case you were wondering.

Follow Gemma at
www.gemmacorrell.com
or on Twitter: @gemmacorrell

A Handy Index
of Useful Terms

Being a Girl

Andrews McMeel Publishing
a division of Andrews McMeel Universal
1130 Walnut Street, Kansas City, Missouri 64106

www.andrewsmcmeel.com

First published in Great Britain by Hot Key Books,
a division of Bonnier Publishing Fiction.

16 17 18 19 20 RR2 10 9 8 7 6 5 4 3 2 1

ISBN: 978-1-4494-7797-4

Library of Congress Control Number: 2016939193

Editor: Grace Suh
Art Director: Diane Marsh
Production Editor: Erika Kuster
Production Manager: Carol Coe

ATTENTION: SCHOOLS AND BUSINESSES
Andrews McMeel books are available at quantity discounts with bulk
purchase for educational, business, or sales promotional use. For information,
please e-mail the Andrews McMeel Publishing Special Sales Department:
specialsales@amuniversal.com.